THE WORLD
IS YOUR MARKET

THE WORLD
IS YOUR MARKET

John Newlin

Prima Publishing
P.O. Box 1260BK
Rocklin, CA 95677
(916) 786-0426

Production by Janis Paris, Bookman Productions
Copyediting by Cary Groner
Composition by Janet Hansen, Alphatype
Interior design by Suzanne Montazer, Bookman Productions
Jacket design: Paul Page Design, Inc.

Library of Congress Cataloging-in-Publication Data

Newlin, John.
 The world is your market / John Newlin.
  p. cm.
 Includes index.
 ISBN 1-55958-439-4
  1. United States—Commerce. 2. Competition,
International. 3. Foreign trade promotion—
United States. I. Title.
HF3031.N49 1994
658.8'48—dc20   93-33154
                CIP

John Newlin consults with companies and speaks to organizations about international issues. You may contact him by writing Newlin Associates, P.O. Box 5104, Westport, CT 06881.

94 95 96 97 98 RRD 10 9 8 7 6 5 4 3 2 1

Printed in the United States of America

To Sandra, Jon, Kim, and Todd,
whose confidence and support never wavered . . . and to all the
wonderful people I've met and worked with around the world.

CONTENTS

ACKNOWLEDGMENTS

Many people deserve and have my gratitude for their support in the development of this book. From a general perspective, I thank the hundreds of business associates, friends, and acquaintances throughout the world with whom I have worked, talked, debated, negotiated, and spent much enjoyable time. This group includes many persons in the U.S. as well, in government, business, think tanks, universities, and elsewhere. The endless experiences all contribute greatly to my current understanding of the world and my views put forward in this book.

More specifically, I must thank Jim Kelly, Ray Weir, Bill Troutman, and Ray Greiner, who read drafts and commented on specific issues from their wealth of experience. Jim Kelly, in particular, was involved early on in offering insights.

I thank my wife Sandra and my daughter Kim for their monumental work in the last days in putting the manuscript in the proper word processing program for the publisher. My son Jon and son-in-law Todd Thode were also rocks of moral support and offered numerous helpful comments. Sandra, especially, has been a strong sounding board in listening to my opinions and offering her reactions.

There are many more friends who gave advice and moral support—and always asked how the book was going—friends such as Jere, Jeanette, Ray, Leslie, Gwynne, Margaret, John, Dave, Jane, Bill, Lynn, Shirley, the gang from Hastings, and more.

The several editors and other publishing staff involved with this book were of great assistance, positive and supportive throughout, always cheery in their calls to see how things were going or to offer helpful comments. Those calls were always welcome, as an author does get lonely. Jennifer, Andi, Karen, Diane, Jenn, Janis, and Cary all contributed greatly.

There are institutions to thank as well. The New York Public Library and the Westport, Connecticut library in particular deserve my thanks—I often used their resources, especially their computer research facilities. Numerous branches of the government supplied material, as did several international organizations; to all these I say thanks.

After all these sincere expressions of gratitude, in the end I take full responsibility for the content of this book. The new international business world is amazing and exciting, and I hope you will find this book supportive in meeting its challenge.

Introduction:
The New
Business World

For years we Americans have lived and operated in our cocoon, secure in the belief that the position to which we leaped at the end of World War II would last forever. We were a "can do" nation, one whose industrial might, entrepreneurship, and hard-working citizenry would ensure that we would always be light years ahead of the rest of the world in standard of living and economic might.

The tiny percentage of Americans and the few American businesses that ventured abroad went to such safe areas as England and perhaps to one or two other places in Europe. Only gigantic multinational corporations such as the oil companies have operated throughout the world for years, joined today by McDonalds, Coca-Cola, and a few similar firms.

Now we are finally realizing that many newly industrialized countries have growth rates that far excel ours, with cities more modern than any in the United States, and with skilled citizens willing to work long and hard to produce higher standards of living. This is not occurring only in Europe, but rather in countries in Asia and the Pacific, Latin America, and a few other areas. At the same time, economic boundaries are falling all over the world. Europe, parts of Asia and the Pacific, and even North America are each moving steadily toward becoming single economic markets, even if political boundaries remain. With the fall of the Soviet Union and the freeing of Eastern Europe, moreover, countless additional opportunities have joined the business arena.

While governments are indeed moving to larger and larger alliances for economic purposes, modern communications and transportation have made "one world" a functional reality. If you are involved in business operations around the world, you can talk by telephone, fax documents back and forth, communicate by electronic mail over computer networks, or jump on an international airliner and visit customers or government officials in person. You can be almost anywhere in the world in twenty-four hours. There may be some countries where communications are still difficult, but these are few, and each day modern communications draw nearer to them as well.

THE CALL OF DISTANT LANDS

By now businessmen and businesswomen have indeed heard repeatedly that we're all living in one world, that it's one big market out there, and that if you are not participating in business outside the United States, you are not only missing out, you are slowly fading away. If that is true, and indeed it seems to be, what's stopping you? Get going!

Getting started is just the problem, isn't it? You know what you should do, but the world is unknown and frightening. Indeed, this is exactly where much of American business is right now . . . in a slow-growth American economy, recognizing that there is real growth "out there," but not knowing how to get involved in it.

For most of the history of this country, the market in the United States was more than big enough to support us. Most of American business has always been focused on domestic markets. Consider that in 1991 export sales accounted for less than 10 percent of the gross domestic product (GDP) of the U.S., whereas they accounted for more than 25 percent of the GDP of Canada and Germany and more than 20 percent of the GDP of Britain, France, and Italy. No other modern industrial country had exports of less than 10 percent of its GDP; the only other countries with as low a percentage as the United States were Brazil, India, Peru, and nine more very undeveloped countries in Africa and Asia.[1]

The great multitude of American firms operates in only a few states, and, for them, even moving to other areas of the country is a big decision. Once a U. S. ambassador to one of the rapidly growing Asian countries remarked to me that getting the companies in his home state to consider opportunities in Asia was not the first challenge—the primary challenge was to get them to consider even looking outside the *state itself.*

Nevertheless, we all are only too familiar with the many business operations in our country from non-American companies. Some of the factories and the real-estate investments are very visible, but the true extent of foreign business activity here is staggering. Japan gets all the press attention, but Britain has investments of a similar magnitude, and Canada as well as other European countries also have a large presence. In truth, most of the industrialized world recognized long ago that this is becoming one economic world, and companies from other countries have been seeking their share of the world market for years. Corporations from Japan and major European countries have been venturing throughout the world with a great deal more support and cooperation from their home governments than has ever existed in the United States, where it is still popular for business and government to argue more than cooperate. Somehow, this exciting new world and its rules have gotten well ahead not only of our companies, but of our entire system of business and government.

BOOMING MARKETS

Here is the real attraction for American companies—*the booming markets out there in other lands.* Many countries of which most Americans have barely heard, and which have long been considered in the "developing country" category, are doing just that. They are actually developing and booming!

Let's look at Asia, the center of the boom. Visitors to Singapore, Kuala Lumpur in Malaysia, or Hong Kong will think they have just landed in a crowded combination of Houston and New York City, with modern skyscrapers everywhere and people moving and working fast, fast, fast! Americans first seeing this may wonder where it all came from. In fact, it's been happening for some time. Enlightened governments recognizing the need for economic growth have fostered environments attractive to foreign investment and business operations, and the world has noticed. Companies from many other highly industrialized countries are very active in these new markets, often with the strong backing of their governments.

A few multinational American companies have noticed and are operating in such places, but not many of the numerous American companies that are large by world standards but not high in the *Fortune* rankings have joined them. Governments of these developing countries know this. A top trade official of an aggressive Asian nation told me not long ago that his country has to get not only the gigantic American companies interested, but also the large, the middle sized, and the small. He is keenly interested in having American companies come to his country.

The most attractive growth economies in the world today are in spots like Singapore, Malaysia, South Korea, and Thailand, countries that for well more than a decade have had real annual economic growth rates in the spectacular 5–10 percent range. There are other attractive areas as well, most recently in Latin American countries such as Chile, Argentina, and—surprising to most Americans who still know the country only through old Western movies—Mexico. Although these countries were not as strong as their Asian counterparts in the eighties (and still are not), they have been taking obvious steps to open their economies to foreign enterprise. Their economies are coming on strong in the nineties with recent real growth rates approaching those of the leading Asian countries.

Consider what real economic growth has been in the U. S. during the same period, or in other countries in which American companies feel most comfortable, such as Britain, Canada, or Australia. Since 1980 the economies of these four nations have had real annual growth rates averaging between 2 and 3 percent, not counting the disastrous showings in the recession of the early nineties, when all dipped below zero.

The prospects for the future look about the same; booming new market opportunities await. Your company does not have to push others aside; it can actually grow with the growth in the market.

Furthermore, you don't have to enter just the top-growing countries. Pick others that are just starting to grow; or if you are really adventuresome and planning for the long run, choose a developing country that is not growing now but seems to be creating the conditions to

start a major upward trend. You might capture a significant market position quickly and then hold it on the rise.

Most countries in the world are in this "developing"
category, but at different points.

There are many possible rewards for going abroad,
both for you and for your organization—profits, market
share, and growth. There are of course real risks, too:
financial risks, people risks, and political risks. Where will
you find qualified people to handle the business or staff its
operations? Will the local country allow you any outside
experts to manage your operation? What are the customs
and local culture like? Can you trust the government? Can
you in fact trust the U. S. government not to do something
that may hurt your business in another country?

THIS BOOK

These are good questions, and we will tackle them all in
this book. However, you already are a businessperson. You
are used to facing risk and uncertainty every day; this is
nothing new, just a change in locale, in names, in milieu.
You are just learning a slightly new game with new players and new rules. Surely you will have tough requirements in the areas of financial oversight, staffing, training,
and interaction with government officials. You will face
different cultures and priorities too, but you may be more
accustomed to such challenges than you know. People in
Texas and people in New York have differences as well!

It is time for American companies to get going. Our
international competition has caught up, and we need to
be out there fighting for our share of the world market.
If not, our economic position is going to slide away from
that of the world players.

Unfortunately, most American companies that would
benefit by seeking international markets are frightened by

the prospect. The large, the middle sized, and the small all share this fear. We do not have the extensive experience of dealing with other cultures and systems that some of the major European industrial nations have.

This book deals with that fear. It is a practical guide to the global business world for executives, managers, and analysts, and also for professors, students, politicians, journalists, and anyone interested in the increasingly interconnected economic world in which we now live. It identifies areas of great business interest, discusses the key factors to be considered in evaluating prospective international involvement, and serves as a friendly guide to establishing successful foreign operations.

For years I have been active in international business as an executive responsible for companies in large regions of the world, as a negotiator in difficult and unusual circumstances, as a developer of new businesses, and as a director in international government/business organizations. Having worked extensively in business and with government and business leaders throughout Asia, Africa, Latin America, the Middle East, and Europe, as well as in the United States, it is clear to me that we must get more involved in the global economy for our own survival.

Most of the comments in this introduction apply also to Canadians, for they too live in a large, modern industrial power far from the diverse mix of countries and societies in Europe, Asia, and Latin America. It must be noted, however, that Canada is a bit more worldly, being a member of the Commonwealth and having a sizable French-speaking population that at times wishes to be independent itself. Perhaps because it is free of the United States' legacy as the dominant country in North America (and for that matter in the world), Canada has been forced to look a bit more outward. Nevertheless, the correct term is "a bit." Canada too must get more active in the international business world to maintain its standard of living in the coming years.

In this book we are going to talk first about various areas you might consider—modern industrialized countries that still offer opportunities, developing countries that are growing rapidly, developing countries that have real potential and seem to be organizing to realize it, those with real potential who are not yet ready to capitalize, and finally those countries to avoid. We will also look at how to find money for these enterprises, how to get profits out and back to the U. S. (after all, there has to be some reason for doing all this), where to find staff, how to manage it, what to look out for, how to find partners, how to survive under unusual political and business pressures, and how to relate to the governments and the people.

We will discuss what you need to know and how you should go about setting up foreign operations, all in straightforward business language. This is a no-holds-barred book. Where there are risks, they are identified in plain language; fortunately, there are many more opportunities than risks.

This is an invigorating time in the business world as well as in life. You have the opportunity to participate in building a new world structure, and your business needs that participation to survive and grow. Whether you just want to sell your wares or participate all the way by having full local affiliate operations, opportunities abound.

By doing all this you can bring home to the U. S. income that would have been lost to companies from other countries. If you do not, the growth will go to Japanese, French, Italian, or British companies, and we will lose our share.

If you are not a businessperson, perhaps this book will excite you to the fascinating new world we all face, and to the challenges ahead. At the very least, it should offer you guidance in accomplishing your aims. That's the essence of any successful businessperson: the ability to get things done, and to do them well.

Talking, thinking too much, being afraid of the future, postponing decisions, and turning inward—these will put you out of business. That approach did not build the greatest country the world has ever seen and certainly will not keep it moving.

The time is now; the world is ready. Are we?

1

Lots of Choices: Ranking the Countries in Attractiveness

Let's face it: There is no easy way to look at the approximately two hundred countries in the world and quickly pick out the right ones for you or your company, especially if, like most business people, you have spent your life focusing on the domestic market.

Nevertheless, it's not as difficult as you may imagine. There are places you must consider and some to avoid absolutely. Between these extremes, countries tend to fall into categories of relative attractiveness. The ranking in this chapter is based on years of doing business in about fifty countries, personal contacts with political and business leaders throughout the world, and a review of the opinions and insights of countless associates in business and in "think tanks" who deal with the international community. This chapter provides a critical overview of geographic areas of interest in today's business world. The following chapters focus on specific factors you must examine for any country you are considering.

Before turning to the categories, let us recognize two basic trends in the world today; the first is a seeming consistency of development throughout large geographic regions, and the second is the fall of economic boundaries between many countries with the establishment of huge international trading blocs. Keep these trends in mind as you consider any country and its unique attractiveness.

From the geographic perspective, the Asia–Pacific Rim area holds the most rapidly developing economies in the world. This designation, which we'll shorten to "Asia/Pac Rim," refers to countries in Asia and on (or with easy access to) the Pacific Ocean, as well as those island nations in the Pacific. Nations in this area seem to be getting the formula right and are joining the march to becoming full-fledged modern industrial societies. Of course, this is not true for all countries in Asia, and some still languish far behind.

Next to Asia/Pac Rim, Latin America is the most attractive area, with great prospects for growth and development. Several countries there are already off and running, and are among the highest-rated prospects, although Brazil, the largest one, remains well behind.

At the other extreme, Africa, a continent of more than fifty countries, ranks last in current economic standing and in prospects for the future. Isolated examples of economic potential exist, but overall there is a real possibility that Africa will fall even farther behind in the coming years.

Between these extremes is Western Europe, which is moving steadily to become one economic "country" larger than the United States. Thousands of highly educated people have been working in Brussels and elsewhere for several decades to create a unified Europe, which will be an economic and political powerhouse. Officially this unified economic market became a reality on January 1, 1993, although the many problems related to currency and the convergence of economic policies of the participating countries have yet to be ironed out. Many French citizens remain fearful of losing their national sovereignty, and the same goes for the British, the Danes, and others, but the process is marching inexorably forward.

In the U. S. we now have an economic trade agreement with Canada and Mexico. The North American Free Trade Agreement (NAFTA) establishes the continent as one giant market. At the same time, South American countries have been signing trade agreements with each other, and some anticipate eventually joining an expanded NAFTA.

The rest of the world has noticed these activities. Singapore, Malaysia, Thailand, Japan, and others are concerned about these new economic groups, and are thinking about forming one of their own. ASEAN, the Association of Southeast Asian Nations—an organization including Singapore, Malaysia, Thailand, Indonesia, Brunei, and the Philippines—has embarked on a program of steadily reducing tariffs affecting trade among member countries, in addition to its other activities. The relevant point for business regarding such trading blocs is that operation in one member country usually opens the entire bloc to a company's products; conversely, failure to operate in any member country may subject a company's exports into the bloc to difficult competitive burdens such as high tariffs or even problems of access.

Then there are Eastern Europe and the former Soviet republics. This giant area is well behind Asia and Latin America in current business attractiveness, and ahead of only Africa; for a few spots even that may be debated. In the long term—and that means many years—natural resources, large total population, and geographic size all make this area extraordinarily interesting. Surprisingly to some, a few countries in Eastern Europe are ahead of the former Soviet republics. Poland, the Czech Republic, and Hungary seem to be turning the corner from low economic performance in the beginning of the 1990s, and may be ready for more positive results. In the years since the fall of the Soviet bloc and the freeing of Eastern Europe, the economies of all these countries crashed, but now the Eastern European countries show signs of turning around, even though the jury is clearly out on the former members of the Soviet Union.

With all this background, we are now ready to turn to the rankings. Countries are grouped into five categories for their overall attractiveness to American business activity (the countries are not ranked within the categories). A country not included in one of these more "attractive" groupings may nevertheless be perfect for you or your company if it offers what you are looking for. Natural-resource availability, an inexpensive labor pool, proximity to key markets, and cheap hydroelectric power are examples of benefits that may render an unattractive country appealing to a particular company. Not all countries in the world appear in this ranking, but this should provide a basis for considering where your interests lie. (Table 1-5 at the end of this chapter provides a quick appraisal of desirable qualities for the countries in the top four groups. The last category, that of countries to avoid, is not included in the table, as there are few promising attributes to point out.)

WINNERS: THE SOLIDLY GROWING DEVELOPING COUNTRIES

This is the cream of the crop; countries with economically enlightened governments that encourage foreign investments, with rapidly growing economies, and with hard-working citizens.

There really are such places. Number one on any list is *Singapore*. This nation has clearly dedicated itself to being

TABLE 1-1   Annual % Real Economic Growth[1]

	1990	1991	1992
Chile	2	6	10
Hong Kong	3	3	5
Malaysia	10	9	8
Mexico	4	4	3
Saudi Arabia	12	2	6
Singapore	8	7	6
South Korea	9	8	5
Taiwan	5	7	7
Thailand	10	8	7

a business mecca, recognizing that booming business means an improved standard of living for its citizens. The government works with prospective businesses to make the situation as attractive as possible. Singapore has an Economic Development Board (EDB) and a Trade Development Board (TDB) staffed by people eager to work with you. Both the EDB and the TDB have representatives in the U.S. to counsel American companies in the development of their business in and with Singapore (these offices and similar facilities for other countries are included in the Appendix, with appropriate contact information.)

Singapore has had a real average annual growth in its economy of about 7 percent since 1980. The country is eager to attract American investment and is looking for midsized companies as well as larger ones. It serves as a distribution hub for the ASEAN region and gains you entry to the ASEAN markets.

Singapore, however, is high on everyone's list; this is a "discovered" country. The U.S. government has been in discussion with Singapore for some time regarding improving trade arrangements, and there may eventually be a formal trade agreement between the U.S. and all the ASEAN countries, or perhaps between North America and ASEAN.

Just next door is the much larger *Malaysia,* which has
many of the advantages of Singapore and a larger population. Kuala Lumpur, the capital, is a modern business
center. The government is willing to work with you, but
there are interesting side issues. The country is populated
largely by Moslems and by Chinese. The Moslems as a
group are referred to as "bumiputras," or just as "bumis."
The Chinese have been so successful at their business efforts that the government has found it necessary to come
to the aid of the bumis, and various provisions favor them
in areas such as hiring and staffing; this is reminiscent of
the affirmative-action programs in the U.S. (new condo-
miniums carry a lower price for bumi buyers than for others, for example).[2]

Thailand is another country in this category, although
it should possibly be moved to the section for countries
with potential that are still getting prepared. The economy has grown at about 8 percent annually since 1980.
This country is really ready to go. The government, however, can be unpredictable. Thailand flirts with real
democracy, but there are occasional coups; nevertheless,
the country seems to have a sincere drive for a stable government to support the boom that has been building for
some time. The business center is the giant city Bangkok,
which has perhaps the worst traffic in the world and a
serious pollution problem.

South Korea is a true tiger, a booming economy with
hardworking citizens and real energy. There are a few concerns, however, the most troublesome being restrictions
on U.S. ownership and participation in certain industries.
Prospects for eventual reunification with North Korea,
slim though they may be at present, make long-term
investments potentially even more attractive, as a unified
Korea would be an economic giant.

Hong Kong is currently a business enigma. Governed as
a center of capitalism, this city has prospered for many

years. In 1997, Britain will give this city back to the People's Republic of China (PRC), and despite reassurances from the Chinese, the future of Hong Kong remains uncertain. Best bets are that the PRC will allow Hong Kong to continue to operate as a special economic zone within China, serving as a window to the business world for the country. Hong Kong currently serves as a financial and shipping center and very definitely a comfortable way into China for American business. In reality Southern China and Hong Kong already function much like one economic zone.

With the uncertainty posed by 1997, many Hong Kong citizens who have the means have been seeking dual citizenship in other countries or have been emigrating outright to such places as the United States, Canada, Malaysia, and Singapore. Some local Hong Kong corporations themselves are moving their headquarters elsewhere. As part of the Immigration Act of 1990, the U.S. has permitted an increased number of Hong Kong citizens to obtain a visa but remain in Hong Kong for several years, thereby allowing them to test the post-1997 environment.[3]

Taiwan (previously Formosa, or old Nationalist China, as it used to be called), also falls into this category. A concern is its proximity to the PRC, and the latter's strongly held belief that it owns this island nation. Nevertheless, the situation is stable for now.

Chile is also in this category. Americans have trouble forgetting the days of former leader Pinochet, but despite his repressive behavior, the economy did well and the country is economically sound. The current president has taken steps toward reassuring the world about the stability and character of Chile's democracy, and this is a very good place to do business. Santiago is a beautiful city, clean beyond most Americans' wildest dreams (I've never forgotten the sight of workers scrubbing park benches at dawn). Chile has pressed the U.S. government for years to begin bilateral trade negotiations, and it conceivably could be brought into NAFTA eventually.

Mexico is probably the biggest surprise member of this club. Most Americans would be shocked to see the recent economic growth of the country. President Salinas and his predecessor have taken giant strides to remove the shadier sides of Mexican political and business tradition and to put this nation on a firm footing for the nineties and beyond. This is a giant in the making.

Mexico is the eleventh-largest country in the world in population. With the new North American Free Trade Agreement opening further the already wide-open door between the U.S. and Mexico, the sky is the limit for Mexican businesses and for Americans who choose to operate or to sell there.

Even before the passage of NAFTA, Mexico took steps to greatly reduce Mexican duties on imported U.S. goods. The U.S. enjoys a positive trade balance with Mexico. President Salinas is serious, as is his administration. He and many of his cabinet officials are in their forties and have graduate degrees from the top schools in the world. The Salinas administration, at least the president and his cabinet, have a reputation as the best and brightest in the world. Unfortunately, under Mexican law, Salinas cannot run for reelection, so in 1994 the country will choose another leader. Nevertheless, you must consider Mexico if you are in business in the United States.

Saudi Arabia is included in this top category because of its vast oil wealth and because American firms have already benefited by building plants or other structures there, and by selling needed goods. Its economic performance is more erratic than others in this category because it is so closely tied to the price of oil. Saudi Arabia has a close relationship to the U.S., as was demonstrated in the Gulf War, and this connection should continue. Nevertheless, the culture and the system are difficult for

Americans and require patience, perseverance, and care. Women are subjected to tight dress codes and behavior requirements that are oppressive to anyone from a Western environment. The country bans alcohol and all religions other than Islam. Anyone contemplating business here should be warned that relationships are always difficult to negotiate and to continue. Saudis take extreme positions in negotiations and stick to them.

MODERN INDUSTRIAL COUNTRIES WITH OPPORTUNITIES

Table 1-2 lists ten modern industrial countries with solid business opportunities, although their more mature economies clearly are not growing at the dramatic rates of the countries in the previous section.

Portugal is a top candidate. The country has lower costs than most of Europe and high labor productivity, and will be highly competitive in the European Community (E.C.).

TABLE 1-2   Annual % Real Economic Growth[4]

	1990	*1991*	*1992*
Australia	1	2	2
Britain	1	(2)	(1)
Canada	1	(2)	1
France	2	1	1
Germany	5	3	1
Japan	5	4	2
New Zealand	(1)	0	1
Portugal	4	2	1
Spain	4	2	1
U.S.	1	(1)	2

Spain is similar to Portugal, but larger and further along in development. Both Spain and Portugal have had real economic growth averaging about 3 percent annually for more than a decade, but a significant growth opportunity for these countries is unfolding now, as the E.C. truly takes effect. The lower labor and manufacturing costs in Portugal and Spain make products from these countries highly competitive in the European Community.

The entire E.C. is a market opportunity, of course, as far as selling goods and services, but Portugal and Spain are leading candidates for the location of operations. Remember, most of Europe has a mature economy much like that of the U.S., and only slow, steady growth can be expected overall. The breaking of economic borders does, however, bring opportunities for synergistic combinations of companies throughout the continent. The implication for an American firm having an operation in one member state is that it should be able to market from that state throughout Europe just as any other European company. (For example, an American plant selling from the U.S. into an E.C. country may have a duty disadvantage versus a competitive Italian plant selling the same item from Italy into that country, but an American-owned plant in Belgium should be able to escape this.)

Germany remains the economic giant of Europe. Its attention now and for the next several years, however, is turned toward absorbing and building up the former East Germany. This is a world leader whose skills and financial resources are being strained, although the country is no doubt equal to the challenge.

Britain continues to have problems adjusting to the new world, never quite knowing to what extent it wishes to be a part of the E.C. Its need for jobs may offer situations attractive to American firms. (Throughout this book "Britain" is used to refer to the United Kingdom.)

France too will no doubt prosper and provide opportunities of the sort to be found in other mature econ-

omies. Similar comments apply to the Scandinavian countries and to *Switzerland,* lands of extraordinarily high per
capita income.

Canada always has opportunities, but you must seek
them out. Like the U.S. and most of the modern countries
of Europe it is growing slowly overall. On the positive side,
it is a member of NAFTA, its currency is relatively stable,
most of its people speak English, and it is an easy first
move outside the U.S. Canada is also the largest trading
partner of the U.S.

As is well known, the province of Quebec is a bit independent in Canada, being the home of French-speaking
people who have often desired separation from the rest
of the country. Quebec may not be quite as friendly to
Americans as the rest of Canada, but then this is another
good first test; you don't think that all the world receives
Americans with open arms, do you? (Actually, to a great
extent, it does. My experience in all continents is that
Americans usually are well-liked, especially in many developing countries.)

Japan's economic boom was the precursor of the current explosion in other Asia/Pac Rim nations. It now has
one of the three largest economies on earth and could
easily become the largest by the end of this decade. Its
future is tied very much to the economic health of the
other giants, and it is probably too big and mature to be
able to experience Singapore-like growth for an extended
period. There are more attractive investment areas than
Japan, but this is a nation of newly wealthy people. Some
American companies have been successful here—for example, Exxon and Mobil. American companies that have
something Japan really needs or wants seem to do well. It's
not an easy entry candidate, but this is a monstrous economy with lots of money.

Australia and *New Zealand* are favored by Americans
because we all speak English and have a similar heritage.
Nevertheless, their economies aren't growing fast, they

have small populations, and both have a more socialist approach to economic affairs than Americans are used to. Business entries should be in areas of local need where a true niche can be found. These two countries perhaps should not be included in such a lofty category, but their governments are stable, they do have a solid history of private business, their citizens like Americans, and they certainly should be expected to grow in population in the coming years.

The U.S. would of course be included in this category.

NEAR WINNERS: DEVELOPING COUNTRIES WITH REAL POTENTIAL THAT ARE ORGANIZING TO REALIZE THAT POTENTIAL

Table 1-3 presents six large developing countries of great potential that are preparing for future economic growth.

China is the primary entry in this group; no place has more potential. One fifth of the world lives there. Despite the repressive image the government left in people's minds as a result of the Tiananmen Square incident, the country is steadily moving to allow more private business initiatives for its citizens, as well as on the part of foreign investors. In 1997 it gets the added boost of regaining Hong Kong.

China likes foreign companies that bring the technology it needs. This is a carrot that American companies can always offer in negotiations for attractive deals. As a businessman involved in manufacturing in China recently told me, the country much prefers being taught how to make something to being sold the finished product. In his

TABLE 1-3   Annual % Real Economic Growth[5]

	1990	*1991*	*1992*
Argentina	0	5	9
Brazil	(4)	1	(1)
China	5	7	12
India	6	4	1
Indonesia	6	6	6
South Africa	(1)	(1)	(2)

words, the country would rather learn how to fish than be sold fish.

China also likes foreign investors whose business operations will bring U.S. dollars or other easily convertible world currencies that the country desperately needs (that is, "hard" currencies). Its own money is one of the soft currencies that we will discuss in Chapter 5. Such currency is not worth much on the world stage; China needs hard currency to buy goods from other countries. An interested business could manufacture in China and sell the merchandise abroad, thereby utilizing inexpensive local labor and benefiting itself and the country with hard-currency receipts.

There is real political risk here, of course, as there is always a chance the successors to China's aging leaders may indeed include one or more reactionaries who dislike the West. There is also risk from the U.S. government; disputes between the White House and Congress may lead to trade restrictions against a country unpopular in the American press. Affiliates of U.S. companies in foreign lands have to watch for such restrictions, and we will discuss this issue in Chapters 11 and 12. Despite these concerns, some American companies are active in China, for example, Motorola.[6] One reason is that labor is extraordinarily inexpensive there. The real growth in the economy has been amazing; with an annual average from 1980 to 1990 approaching 10 percent. Of course, the original base was small indeed.

Argentina is another country moving rapidly to realize its potential. At one time, Argentina was among the largest industrial countries in the world, and it is showing signs of wanting to reclaim such a position. The government has taken enormous steps to privatize government-held industries and get inflation under control. There is still a ways to go, but this country is on the move and is seeking to join Chile and Mexico as economic success stories in Latin America. This is an opportunity to get involved early in a sophisticated nation whose organization and priorities were confused for many years, but now seem to be clearing up. You will, it should be noted, have to deal with a male macho culture stronger than most in the world. Nevertheless, Argentina is a nice place, one in which Americans can feel at home, especially if they speak Spanish.

South Africa belongs either here or in the following category. This is the only country in Africa with significant economic potential. It has the infrastructure, the skills, and the knowledge to succeed. It also has human-rights problems of the greatest magnitude, and your assessment of them will guide your consideration. It does appear, however, that the country is moving slowly forward in dealing with human-rights concerns, and is therefore an interesting proposition. If the country continues to advance and does reach a peaceful internal settlement, it has the wherewithal to dominate the African continent, or at least the southern half. It's a bit riskier than the other countries in its class, but positioning an operation there might bode well for the long term.

As we all know too well, political risk is high regarding not only actions of the South African government, but those of other groups within the country, and indeed those of the U.S. government, which in the past has placed crippling restrictions on U.S. companies operating there. Those restrictions have now largely been lifted, although many state and local governments in the U.S. continue to carry such laws.

The following three countries are included in this category although they surely could have easily fallen into the next one. They are truly on the borderline, with enormous potential but troublesome questions.

Indonesia is a major population center, having more than 180 million people (fourth in the world); it also has abundant natural resources and a variety of opportunities. It is in the midst of the booming Asia/Pac Rim region and has shown promising economic growth in recent years. It should eventually join the fast track on which its neighbors, Singapore, Malaysia, and Thailand, have been riding. Nevertheless, the country can be risky because the government is not so open for foreign business activity.

Similarly, *India* is a giant in terms of population, second in the world with 800 million people. It has been difficult for foreign business to gain a foothold, however, as the government still restricts foreign investment; nevertheless, there have been recent steps toward relaxing the restrictions. An added difficulty is the increase in tension between the majority Moslem population and the sizable Hindu population. Nevertheless, the country's economy is indeed growing—as is Indonesia's—with both economies having a real rate of annual increase of about 5 percent since 1980. Just as with China, the U.S. business world cannot ignore such a potentially huge market as it struggles to move more into the economic mainstream. China and India together contain almost 40 percent of the earth's inhabitants.

Then there is *Brazil.* This country is everyone's candidate for a nation that should be an economic boomer but is not. Brazil is the fifth-most-populous nation on earth. Its people have the talent and skills to make anything (and they do), but the country also has had for years thoroughly unreliable currency, fiscal policy, and government.

It is easy for a visitor to be enticed by Brazil, but beware. Successful operations here require nimble financial wizardry in areas not often encountered by Americans. Foreign business operations do indeed succeed, but decisions must be made in light of constantly changing currency values and interest rates, both of which vary in amounts far beyond any American's experience. As an example of the speed of such change, the 1990 annual inflation rate in Brazil was nearly 3,000 percent, and it returned to that level in mid-1993. The nation is beautiful, as large as the continental U.S., and bursting with potential, but it also has terrible poverty, high crime, and a seeming disregard for the welfare of its citizens as a whole. Despite its great potential, there are no overwhelming signs that this country is on the right economic road, and it could have easily slipped into the next category.

UNREALIZED POTENTIAL: DEVELOPING COUNTRIES WITH REAL POTENTIAL THAT ARE NOT YET ON THE RIGHT ROAD

Table 1-4 presents countries in an intriguing category. These countries are recognized as having obvious potential, some even great potential; but they currently have difficulty realizing it. If this chapter is revised in a couple of years, perhaps one or two of these will be upgraded.

Colombia is certainly a candidate for a higher ranking, with its steadily attractive economic performance. There is, however, one serious question: Why would you want to get involved in the center of the international drug world?

TABLE 1-4   Annual % Real Economic Growth[7]

	1989	1990	1991
Botswana	13	5	9
Colombia	3	4	2
Czech Republic/			
Slovakia	1	(2)	(16)
Hungary	(2)	(7)	(9)
Poland	(2)	(10)	(6)
Egypt	3	3	2
Ghana	5	3	5
Nigeria	7	8	4
Philippines	6	2	(1)
Former Soviet			
Republics	2	(2)–(5)	(10) est.
Zimbabwe	4	4	4

The *Philippines* is another nation seemingly not going anywhere. The Filipino people have the skills to do anything; they build and operate complex manufacturing plants in the Middle East and throughout the world. They staff the entertainment industry in many areas of the world and fill many basic service positions, but all because the economy at home just doesn't support them.

It is difficult to understand how this country, which has so much talent, missed the economic boom in which its neighbors such as Singapore and Malaysia are prospering, but it did. Part of the explanation lies in a history of unenlightened government and extensive corruption. This country could benefit from a Salinas, but then so could Brazil and many other nations. The Philippines has lots of people, a great deal of talent, and plenty of natural beauty, but is basically going nowhere for now.

In Eastern Europe, *Poland, Hungary,* and the new *Czech Republic* and *Slovakia* (formerly Czechoslovakia) were recently freed from Soviet control; their people possess some knowledge of the private approach to business and are eager to build their nation's economies to higher levels. Many of them have also been the beneficiaries of educational systems strong in mathematics, science, and engineering. One aggressive city in Hungary recently claimed that of its work force of 140,000, three-fourths have been trained in technical colleges.[8] It is nevertheless important to remember that these countries have been under communist control for so long that there will be a slow evolution of modern business knowledge and an equally slow development of institutions to support operations. These are the leading candidates in Eastern Europe, together with the former East Germany (now part of Germany).

The former Soviet nations could have been included in the category of countries to avoid, but they are grouped here because of their long-term potential. There is a need for a major education effort. Private capitalism and survival in a world in which the government does not provide all basic needs in life, including jobs and housing, is new and frightening to the citizens. The legal system is a quagmire, it is difficult to get money out, there are an extraordinary number of ethnic groups and languages, there is a real need to engage in barter trade (discussed in Chapter 5), and the area has eleven time zones. What a mess. When a contingent of Russian businesspeople visited Iowa, among the most difficult concepts to communicate was how a commercial bank works and the nature of a commercial loan.

These are, however, big countries with lots of people and abundant natural resources. If a company really wants to try to operate there, it will need time, patience, training for local employees, and managers with great creativity who can think on their feet, much like the requirements for managers of foreign affiliates in African countries.

Few of the many countries in Africa fall into this category; most are best to avoid. Unfortunately for most of

Africa, after independence was gained from European colonial powers during the past thirty-five years, there were many experiments with dictatorships and some form of socialism. Capitalism and democracy as practiced by the West were scorned by the early leaders after independence, many of whom ran the countries for their personal benefit. Some still do. This approach ran the countries' economies into the ground.

With the rebirth of freedom in the former Soviet bloc (which had been the benefactor of some of the more outrageous African regimes), and with the support of such financial institutions as the International Monetary Fund (IMF) and the World Bank, which seek to encourage private enterprise, change is taking place.

Any consideration of operating in Africa must take into account the necessity of working with difficult regimes, different cultures, stiff training needs, and harsh environments. On the positive side, the opportunity exists to establish your company in a major market position as an enterprise possibly vital to a particular country. Accordingly, some governments are willing to negotiate attractive terms for foreign operations.

Zimbabwe has natural resources and the great beauty that could support a large tourism industry. The government seems to be taking the steps needed to recognize the guarantees, real or implied, that must be given to Western companies for them to invest significantly, such as the right to repatriate dividends. Zimbabwe's neighbor *Botswana* is stable and attractive, but its population and economy are very small.

You might think *Kenya* should fall into this category; unfortunately, it is not so attractive to American investment these days. There is a degree of instability in the government, and it has been difficult to repatriate funds.

Ghana is slowly improving from the near disaster it was in 1980, and its economy has grown at an average annual rate of 3 percent since then. The IMF and the World Bank are using Ghana as a showcase, so there is some support for business efforts here.

Other possibilities are *Egypt* and *Nigeria.* Egypt is among the Arab–African nations in North Africa in which the culture is different than in the rest of the continent. There are, however, no booming economies there either. American investments in Egypt, nevertheless, benefit from the close relationship between the U.S. and Egypt, and the high level of U.S. foreign aid means there should always be dollars available in the economy to send dividends back home. Nigeria is the seventh-largest country in the world in population and is struggling to get back to democracy. Under anyone's assessment, this is a difficult country, and should probably be avoided until clearer signs of improvement in stability, security, and integrity can be seen.

COUNTRIES TO AVOID

The world changes overnight, as we have seen in the Soviet Union, so the following countries hopefully will not always be in this section.

Zaire is a large nation rich in natural resources, and has an environment that supports lush vegetation growth. It also is desperately poor, and the government is not stable or consistent. There are too many headaches and risks.

The *Sudan, Somalia,* and *Ethiopia* are characterized by poverty, danger, and risk. Until the military forces of the United States and the United Nations arrived, Somalia was in anarchy. The Sudan is poor and engaged in an internal religious war. Ethiopia just got over a disastrous war but the extent of its recovery remains unclear.

Peru may eventually come out of this category as the current government tries to make headway against terrorists and the highly unstable economy. Unfortunately, the drug world is very much a part of this country too.

Cuba, and *North Korea* are countries where you cannot be in business. The decision is easy, because Uncle Sam says so. *Vietnam* is similarly restricted, but the U.S. government is gradually relaxing the rules for participation of American business. Companies from France, Japan, and many other countries are already actively involved there.

Liberia continues in the throes of civil war, and is very dangerous.

Mozambique is a place of beauty, resources, and size, but it is also extremely dangerous. If the war there is truly over, it will deserve a close watch.

If your company has something of significant value to offer, it is possible to structure an attractive deal with any country, even in this category. Nevertheless, the pain and risk, both financial and physical, in some of the places noted in this last category cannot be overstated.

CONCLUSION

From a business and economic-development standpoint, we are living in the age of Asia. Most probably, we are also living in the early dawning of the age of Latin America, accompanied by a struggle for economic rebirth in Eastern Europe. It is a world with which most Americans and American businesses are not familiar, but it is our present and our future. This is the world in which we will live, work, enjoy life, and prosper. Now, it is time to turn to the issues you must consider as you examine specific opportunities.

Table 1-5 provides a comprehensive appraisal of the countries in the top four categories discussed in this chapter.

**TABLE 1-5   Country Attractiveness for Business
(Countries are not ranked within a category)**

	Economic performance	Economic outlook	Political stability	Government attitude	Financial stability
Winners					
Chile	A	A	A	A	A
Hong Kong	A	B	B	A	A
Malaysia	A	A	A	A	A
Mexico	B	B	A	A	A
Saudi Arabia	B	B	A	A	A
Singapore	A	A	A	A	A
South Korea	A	A	B	B	A
Taiwan	A	A	B	B	A
Thailand	A	A	B	A	A
Modern industrial countries with opportunities					
Australia	B	B	A	A	A
Britain	B	B	A	A	A
Canada	B	B	A	A	A
France	B	B	A	A	A
Germany	B	A	A	A	A
Japan	A	A	A	A	A
New Zealand	C	B	A	A	A
Portugal	A	A	A	A	A
Spain	A	A	A	A	A
USA	B	B	A	A	A
Near winners					
Argentina	B	B	B	A	B
Brazil	C	B	B	B	C
China	A	A	B	B	B
India	A	A	B	B	B
Indonesia	A	A	B	B	B
South Africa	B	B	B	A	A

TABLE 1-5

	Economic performance	Economic outlook	Political stability	Government attitude	Financial stability
Unrealized potential					
Botswana	A	A	B	B	B
Colombia	B	B	C	B	B
Czech Republic	C	C	B	B	C
Hungary	C	C	B	B	C
Poland	C	C	B	B	C
Egypt	B	B	B	B	B
Former Soviet Union	C	C	C	B	C
Ghana	B	B	B	B	B
Nigeria	A	B	C	B	B
Philippines	B	B	B	B	B
Zimbabwe	B	B	B	C	B

Note:
- Economic performance relates to average annual gross domestic product growth, 1987–92

- Government attitude refers to the investment and tax laws and policies affecting foreign business operations in the country, the ease of repatriation of dividends, and the ease of obtaining work permits for foreign staff

- Financial stability refers to the control of inflation and devaluation, and the ease of convertibility of local currency into U.S. dollars
- Economic outlook refers to 1994–2000

A = Above average
B = Average
C = Below average

2

JUST HOW DIFFERENT?

In your international investigations you will find places where employees never disagree with a supervisor, people eat foods that make your stomach crawl, women are truly seen and not heard, cordial office environments do not exist, corruption and graft seem to be ingrained in all facets of life, and much, much more.

The world is not homogeneous. Recognizing the differences, deciding which ones are important and which are superficial, and learning how to relate effectively is key to your success in business abroad. American executives on foreign soil, as well as those back at the home office who must work with the foreign government and business leaders, will face cultural, moral, and communication dilemmas they likely have never before encountered. In this chapter we will explore some of the more enjoyable challenges and some of the serious ones.

Although apprehension is understandable, you should be careful not to blow cultural differences out of proportion. My experience is that people who are sensitive to others and their reactions usually fare well with only a basic background education in the host country's cultures and traditions. For those of us not so sensitive, however (and many business people fall into this category), developing a feel for these differences is a challenge.

How People View the World and Americans

People in other countries may not see the world as you do. In large countries residents have great difficulties looking beyond their borders, just as in the U.S. A friend in Virginia related the story of a co-worker who mentioned to a customer that he was from India.

"Where is that?" the customer asked.

"In Asia," the Indian answered.

"Where is that?" the customer asked.

Sometimes, you wonder just how far our country has to go to operate successfully in this new world.

Brazil is similarly self-centered, as are China, Russia, and India. Australia is also, to an extent. Like the U.S., all of these are geographically enormous countries. In my first time in Brazil several years ago I was struck by how much the educated businesspeople I was with reminded me of Americans. They looked just at Brazil, not at the world, as Europeans tend to do. An amusing incident occurred in a meeting. An American was explaining to the Brazilians how a company in Germany had solved a particular problem.

The Brazilian boss suddenly walked to the map of Brazil and said "Let me show you Germany on this map." He proceeded to draw a tiny circle that was barely visible.

"That is Germany in relation to Brazil," he finished off, pointing out proudly that problems in Brazil might be a tad more extensive.

I once had an experience in Hong Kong that underscores just how little other societies understand of Americans. Hong Kong is one of the really bustling, successful business centers of Asia. I was at lunch in a dim sum restaurant (try one sometime: little trays of various types of dumplings stuffed with all kinds of goodies) with an older Chinese businessman and a couple of younger, well-educated colleagues of his. We were having an enjoyable time and I believe were actually talking about how people in the world don't know much about each other.

As we all began to relax, one of the young businessmen said, with an embarrassed laugh and what seemed to me a real blush, "I don't know how to say this. There is a funny story here in Hong Kong that in the U.S. food for dogs is actually sold in stores!" He laughed again. His manner clearly indicated that he did not believe this to be so and that he was telling me a funny story.

After a moment I replied, "Well, it's true."

"No!" he shouted with amazement and a laugh. "It cannot be!"

We all laughed, and I thought just how incredible this must seem, even in this modern city, that people in the U.S. have so much that stores sell food specifically for dogs. Sometimes Americans do not know where we have come from or what we look like.

Of course, there are countries in which people may be upset with the U.S. for its dominant position regarding some policy. I've had more than a few tough discussions while at social occasions in the Middle East and elsewhere. Even in modern lands abroad, people often have greatly different views of history, events, and culture than we do. One of my earliest discoveries was how well regarded Richard Nixon is all over the world. Foreigners cannot understand why Americans kicked him out of office.

I once was pressed to discuss this through translators at a very formal dinner where I was the only American present. This was in a dictatorship, and I doubt that my comments helped the other guests' understanding very much.

Business executives abroad must also be diplomats. You will probably meet and deal with more officials and businesspeople of that country than members of the U.S. government have ever seen. I still remember my surprise and consternation years ago when I realized how little firsthand experience most State Department people have of the countries with which they work. Often, desk officers in Washington have never been to the country they represent.

There is one other worldview anecdote that really puts us in our place. Once several years ago I was in the People's Republic of China, having lunch with a government guide and another businessman. During the lunch, I was endeavoring to make the usual small talk and relax the situation, which was a bit formal. I asked the government representative, "How many people in China speak English?"

He thought a moment and remarked politely, "Not many."

He continued thoughtfully to eat in silence, then said, "Well, Chinese students are taught English in school." He thought some more about that remark and ate another bite or two. I looked on with interest.

Finally, his eyes brightened as he said, "I guess more people speak English in China than live in the United States."

We all laughed. Years later I told that story in a toast at a dinner in New York honoring some senior politicians from China, and they laughed heartily. It's always good to be the butt of your own joke.

ECONOMIC HISTORY

The economic history of an area bears greatly on local attitudes you will encounter. Americans, Australians, New Zealanders, and Canadians have developed highly successful societies and standards of living in relatively recent times, through hard work and initiative by many people in tough conditions. Although varying in extent, there is an underlying can-do quality to these cultures and to capitalism as practiced in each.

In the former Soviet Union, this history does not exist. For generations the people have lived in state-controlled economies, bought at state-run stores, lived in state-allocated apartments, and worked in state-assigned positions. They have lived in "Big Brother" land. They cannot recall a history of individual entrepreneurship because it did not exist even before the Communists took over, for then the land was under the domination of the czars. The worldview of these people is not that of Americans regarding business and work. Eastern European nations fall somewhere in between, with older citizens recalling private business, and with more understanding of what the new goals are.

African citizens in most countries also do not have applicable backgrounds; for them, survival has been the name of the game. People for the most part have lived off the land and still do. There is extensive craft manufacture, active trading in large bazaars in major cities, and a small level of foreign business investment. Having been freed from domination by foreign colonial powers only in the last few decades, most African countries are still finding their way, developing their own formal government and economic structures and policies. Such societies quite naturally blend aspects of the procedures imposed in the past with their own unique interests and goals.

The Middle East, although now developing from societies that were terribly poor for centuries, does have a visible history of business trade. The *souk,* or open-air bazaar, is pure capitalism in action, with prices for goods set through excited negotiating between seller and buyer. Anyone who has negotiated with Arab businessmen realizes their great skill.

In Western Europe, local employees will likely have objectives similar to those of your employees back home. They seek money, security, and perhaps opportunities for advancement. They will recognize company goals. This is not so for all developing countries, especially the poorer ones. There the individual who is lucky enough to have a position with your operation suddenly has an implied responsibility to help the extended family of which he is a part. That family may include brothers, sisters, parents, cousins, uncles, aunts, and others. The worker may be the one family member with a reliable income. You can imagine that his focus in life likely is not on the increase of company profits but more on helping his family any way he can. Profit maximization and growth in sales volume may be difficult objectives to communicate in such a place. The poorer lands in Asia, Latin America, Eastern Europe, and much of Africa are like this. I suspect that new businesses in the former Soviet states will encounter this as well. The profit motive is not the cornerstone of the world, despite the success of Western capitalism in this century.

There are of course many more such considerations. These, for the most part, are all fun: learning how and what to eat, how to dress, even how to behave in some places. In the Middle East, for example, it is something of an insult to sit with your leg crossed so that the sole of your shoe faces a person. Such conventions can all be learned, and even if they are inconvenient, you can get used to them.

WOMEN IN THE WORKPLACE

There are bigger differences, though, and women's place in society is one of them. The great growth in roles and freedoms for women that has occurred in the U.S. has not happened in most other nations. There is the occasional news story of changes in the role of women in another country, but the U.S. is usually at the forefront of progress.

In the Middle East, especially in the more conservative countries, women play a secondary role in public and business life. In some countries they walk behind the husband, do not talk to strangers, and even keep their faces covered.

In Saudi Arabia, women are generally expected to have their legs and arms always covered. They are not allowed to drive and cannot swim in public pools with their husbands. In such countries, homes may even have two living-room areas so that men may socialize together and women may do so separately. This may sound tough, but in some African, Asian, and even European countries similar situations occur.

In many places in Latin America there is a recognizable male "macho" character to society; Argentina is a good example. Japan, the challenger to the U.S. for world economic leadership, surely is a male-dominated society despite the growing involvement of younger Japanese women. Business entertainment there is not for husbands and their wives; only the men go out together. Japanese bars, which exist in other Asian countries besides Japan, are designed for men. Numerous hostesses in such bars provide conversation and companionship for hardworking executives. Even in some conservative areas in Europe, men and women do not always eat together.

Of course, there are Western European countries in which women actively participate in business and are moving more and more into the work ranks. In other areas I have found a few women working at senior positions, in areas such as Ghana and Zimbabwe. It's important to realize, however, that wherever you go in the world, the U.S. is at the vanguard of the women's movement.

Work Hours and Work Pace

When Western companies began operating in the Middle East, they had to adhere to schedules that closed offices many hours in the heat of the day, reopening later in the evening. Now more and more businesses are adopting the Western work day. Some companies retain the split work day in places along the Mediterranean such as Greece, and in the Middle East.

In countries in which citizens do not have a history of working in factories or offices for eight-hour periods, it will be difficult to build up this tradition. The problem is not just the history but often the weakness of the people. In many countries even healthy citizens are not as physically strong as Americans, due largely to dietary and health-care considerations. Once in the Sudan, I was with a group eating dinner on an outside terrace by the Nile. The Sudanese members of the party were continually anxious regarding the possible presence of flies, in particular the tsetse fly, which carries disease. This of course was a valid concern for all present, but upon later discussion I learned that persons there are already so much weaker than the average American that illnesses that our bodies might fight off could prove fatal to them. The life expectancy in the Sudan is just 51 years. To realize that the Sudan is not unique, consider that the average life expectancy in India is 59, in Bangladesh 52, in Angola 46, and in

Guinea-Bissau 39. Many more countries have such statistics. Life expectancy in the U.S. is 76 years.[1]

In the Sudan the average person takes in about 2,000 calories per day, as compared to more than 3,600 for the typical American, who takes in almost twice as many. It is reasonable to expect that a person's ability to work at a steady pace for a day is affected by the amount of food energy he has consumed. As you might expect, people in the bustling economies of Singapore, Hong Kong, and the like have much higher caloric intakes than people in the Sudan, although still not as high as that of the U.S.[2]

RELIGIOUS CUSTOMS

Another aspect of the work-hour issue relates to religious customs. For example, Moslems must pray five times a day toward Mecca. Conservative Moslems definitely must do this, and work schedules will have to reflect that this may happen at the required times. Imagine what considerations this causes for manufacturing operations, especially continuous-process industries that must always be monitored, and those dealing with dangerous equipment. Provisions have to be made to cover the sensitive procedures and controls.

Not all nations are tolerant of all religions. As previously mentioned, in Saudi Arabia there is only one recognized religion, Islam.

SECURITY AND HEALTH

Concerns in this area are very real but should not be overstated. When the subject has come up in groups of

Americans, I have often remarked that life in the U.S. is more dangerous than anywhere else in the world. That is largely true from the standpoint of crime, but not for those countries at war or with serious health hazards. This subject is the focus of Chapter 13.

CULTURAL CONCERNS IN CHOOSING THE TOP MANAGER

Who should be the top manager of an American operation in a foreign land is a subject at the heart of the cultural-differences issue. In the more modern countries there may be local citizens with the requisite talent. Even in more difficult nations it may be possible to train people over time.

The presence of a local citizen at the top provides visibility with the local business and political leaders. It also brings the corporation greater understanding of local culture and systems. Unfortunately, it also probably gives an individual divided loyalties, because he or she will often have to think of the trade-off in decisions between what is best for the company and what is best for the country. Even if the top local manager remains truly loyal to the company, he may not be able to act on this loyalty, as there may be undue pressure brought to bear on him from the local government. This worry is especially real in third-world countries in which dictators exercise unusual powers. A foreigner in the top spot may be better able to avoid this pressure, but not necessarily, as discussed in Chapter 12.

The foreigner should be an expert from the parent company who clearly brings great knowledge of the company and the industry, and of management organization and techniques. In most countries it would be almost impossible to find a qualified local individual to run your operation in the early years, for he or she would not have the necessary company background. If the operation is to have a top manager from outside the country, an American operation should ideally have an American manager and not one from another country. My experience is that foreign governments react favorably to an American top manager for an American operation and wonder why someone of another nationality, such as a European, would be used. A possible exception to this use of an American would occur in a country where current political turmoil might make him a ripe target for political terrorists, as noted in Chapter 13.

FOOD

Nothing defines a culture more than its food and the style in which it is eaten. Wherever you are in your foreign business dealings, you will doubtless be involved in dinners and receptions involving the local cuisine and culture. Many countries, especially in the developing world, will be very gracious in entertaining during business negotiations.

You should of course look upon this as one of the enjoyable features of your business efforts, and as a wonderful way to get to know the people with whom you are dealing. I should warn you, though, that it is often the custom to give the senior guest at such an affair a special local delicacy. This probably will be a delight, but such items can be a challenge to an American's constitution.

In the Philippines at a gathering, I was once offered a *balut* to eat. *Balut* is a duck embryo still in the egg shell (although fortunately cooked). All eyes in the crowded room turned toward me, and as I was in the process of building up a relationship with all those present, I indeed proceeded to eat it, to a loud round of cheers. In retrospect, I attribute my eating the *balut* also to the ample homemade brandy one of the secretaries had served earlier in the festivities. Shocking? Well, I survived with no ill effects, and years later when I met some of the Filipinos at a conference in another country, one of them asked me, "Do you remember when you ate the *balut?*" and smiled broadly.

It was a relationship cementing step.

Be warned, however, that you do not want to injure yourself or to get ill by trying something strange or frightening. Passing out or throwing up in the midst of those you are dealing with is not an awe-inspiring step. I have found that being from abroad lets you hide behind being a foreigner when necessary. You can use it as an excuse, and almost everywhere the locals, if they are interested in you at all, will relent in their request that you eat something strange; of course, you will not gain the advantage I received from the *balut*.

CORRUPTION AND MORALITY

Other cultural differences include the difficult areas of corruption and morality. In many countries American businesspeople will encounter pressure that they might perceive as some type of corrupt request. This is worrisome in all instances and is especially troubling if the pressure is coming from a political figure or top government official. There are countries in the world where it appears difficult to get any meaningful operation started without such behavior, and if you find this to be true for the country you are interested in, it is time to look elsewhere. The

Foreign Corrupt Practices Act, under which American businesspeople must operate, legally prohibits you from engaging in such pursuits as bribery as well. This area of political pressure, or pressure from society leaders, is perhaps the most serious cultural challenge, and is discussed in depth in Chapters 11 and 12.

The morality issue is difficult to discuss. Honesty as we generally define it in the U.S. may not exist in some cultures. Graft, payoffs, and the like seem to be a way of life in many societies, and some of the newer world leaders are indeed fighting this in an effort to turn their countries around. It is no secret that this is an area on which President Salinas has focused in Mexico, and an area needing attention in places such as Brazil and the Philippines.

Americans in certain lands will encounter other situations of moral challenge, such as the easy availability of sexual partners. You have to deal with this yourself. I suggest that before you wander to other countries, however, that you understand clearly what your personal beliefs and moral code are, and be prepared for them to be tested, even in prospering economies.

Many more issues of cultural difference could be discussed. One I always like to bring up, to the disgust of my lawyer friends, is that most of the world is not flooded with attorneys, as is the U.S. Of course, they would no doubt maintain that this is only a matter of time, but I have found it refreshing to learn that in many nations business deals are a bit simpler in terms of legal documentation (although I still advise that you retain a local counsel and get his or her advice about anything you sign). As an illustration, let me note that there are places in the world where hundreds of millions of dollars pass through agreements no more that four double-spaced pages in length. Life in this country probably used to be like that. Sometimes it is difficult to tell which is the more developed society.

CULTURAL BACKGROUND AND EDUCATION

There are numerous sources of information to help you
become better aware of the culture of a particular country. Chapter 4 describes the steps that a business should
pursue in investigating a country, and gives many sources
of information that also pertain to the issue of culture. A
wise first step in focusing on cultural considerations is to
visit a large bookstore to see if there are current books
about the country. With the growth in interest in the international business world in the U.S., there will likely be
books regarding aspects of business in a particular country, including its unique cultural features. Much has been
written on doing business in Japan, and there are already
a few books on Mexico and China.

Beyond this, a quick read of the latest world or regional atlas will give some recent background. The embassy or consulate from the country will be happy to
furnish materials and to talk to you. The local university
is another good source, as there may be professors teaching on the country in question or even lecturers or students from that country.

There are numerous business/government trade organizations that provide information about culture as well
as business. These and other sources are listed in the
Appendix.

YOU ARE AN OUTSIDER

The conclusion of all this is readily apparent: You are an
outsider. American laws, customs, and traditions do not
apply. You may have wondered why so many foreigners
you encounter in the U.S. appear so deferential. Now you
know. They don't want to step on any toes, to fall into any

cultural traps. You will understand their position when you travel to other lands. Business and life abroad is usually enjoyable, but it is different, and in some places there are serious traps.

3

How Much Alike?

The last chapter may have you wondering anew whether you should remain isolated at home, hibernating, while the international business world grows for others. I hope you won't. Despite the differences noted, people in the most dissimilar countries have fundamental bonds. If we can learn to operate in different styles and to see through cultural differences (some of which are admittedly shocking on the surface), there is much to recognize.

Family

People everywhere are devoted to their families. Sometimes I believe that the less sophisticated a country is, the more family conscious are its people. In Chapter 2, the role of the extended family in developing countries was noted, together with employees' tendency to do everything possible to aid their extended families. The thought that all a person has should be shared with his uncles, sisters, and cousins may seem strange to Americans, who expect healthy people to provide their own support, but surely the love and devotion that underlies this attitude is not difficult for an American to understand.

In the United States parents often worry about having money for their children's college education, or for buying them a car when they are old enough to drive. In other countries, the parent has the child's interests at heart as well, but the items needed may be food, shelter, clothing, and basic education. It's easy to identify with a parent in such a place.

I recall a woman lawyer from a developing country who was invited to the U.S. for exposure to more lawyers and a wider range of issues. She had a young daughter whom she could not appropriately take care of while in the States, but this posed no problem; the daughter was left to the extended family, where sisters, cousins, and for a time the woman's mother took care of her. It must be very much like life was in the United States in the first half of this century and before, when families lived close together in the same town, and the concept of moving around the country and the world did not exist to the extent it does today.

In Ethiopia even during the recent war, I encountered creative people who were able to get their children out of the country and into schools in the U.S. They had the ability, so they got their children out; to them, family was fundamental.

In Mexico City once at dinner, a Colombian businessman and I listened as a Mexican manager brought up some problems he was having with his teenage daughter. It seemed that his communication with her was largely cut off, in part due to her desire to try acting in the theater, and his absolute refusal to allow this, believing it inappropriate. While guitarists strolled by our street-side table and happy people ate, sang, and walked, we listened with interest. Both of us had daughters who had recently passed through their early teenage years, and with a surprising feeling of warmth, we each offered a suggestion or two in a low-key way. A year or so later in Mexico, I saw this man again, and he brought up the problem with his daughter.

"You know," he said, his eyes sparkling, "I did what you suggested, and it worked. Our relationship is much better now."

We were three fathers from three different countries, but we could just as easily have been three fathers talking in Ohio, North Carolina, or Texas.

HERITAGE

We Americans tend to think the world revolves around us. Even abroad, Americans bring up things that happen in the United States as if the local residents should naturally know about them. It is shocking to Americans to spend time with people of other nations and see their interest in local events and occurrences of which we have no knowledge. I remember being in Egypt with some Egyptian colleagues, and finding out that two of them had been on their country's Olympic team in previous years. I had never done anything like that! In Brazil, a local manager told me about being a Brazilian champion rower as we drove past a lovely lake.

In the Sudan, a manager was concerned about the forthcoming marriage of his child and whether he would have the funds to add a suitable room to his house in which the couple would live, as was expected. An Egyptian friend once told my family about bidding to pay the amount the father of his fiancée thought appropriate as a dowry for his marriage. My friend had followed what he thought was sound bidding practice, starting low with the belief that his future father-in-law would negotiate the amount upward. In fact, the father-in-law-to-be was insulted by the low bid, and the impending marriage almost didn't happen. It took some quick explaining by my friend to resolve the situation. Again, this may be a different world, but we can understand it, for the elements of family and trying to do one's best are present.

Beyond the family, there is pride in the tribe, as in Africa. We have discovered from the problems in the former Yugoslavia that Europe has tribes too. If you as a businessperson are going to operate in an area, you will be well served to first investigate the regional history sufficiently to understand its people, where they come from, and of what groups they consider themselves a part. In Eastern and Central Europe as well as in Africa, national boundary lines do not always reflect the groups with which people most identify; such lines were often drawn by outsiders and do not fit.

RELIGION

Although the previous chapter noted religion as one area of cultural difference between people, keep in mind that people's association with a few basic religions forms a common bond as well. Christianity is the major religion throughout North and South America and Europe— where there is a smaller but visible representation of Judaism and Islam—and it is growing rapidly in Asia and Africa. The Middle East is of course dominated by Islam, with some Christianity where permitted, and Judaism in Israel. In Asia you will also encounter Islam, Buddhism, Hinduism, Shintoism, and others. In Africa you will find Islam and numerous local religions.

GREED AND FEAR

These dark subjects are included because one of my long-time business friends thought they should be. He is right in noting that these two negative forces are everywhere in the world, as they are in the U.S., and I don't think that any country has the market cornered. In the developing countries you will, however, sometimes encounter examples of greed that will boggle even the most insensitive mind, and you will have to deal with them on a personal basis. In countries in which most citizens clearly have almost nothing of material value, there are some of the richest people on earth. Some of these are the dictators of poor nations, some are royalty, and some are just materially wealthy individuals in democracies, such as the upper class in Brazil and other Latin American countries. Brazil has a large poor class, a government that has been incapable of solving the country's economic problems of recent years, and a rich aristocracy that seems to like things as they are; or so is the popular opinion. Every country does not have the same system or priorities as the U.S., and, of course, we have our share of disenfranchised people as well.

Fear is present in a variety of forms. Among the poor in both modern and developing countries, people fear not having enough to eat, lack of shelter or of medical help, and more. In some places people fear the government or war. There are still dictators out there and many local wars still rage, despite the end of the Cold War. People in Zaire, Cuba, North Korea, Angola, the former Yugoslavia, and other areas haven't yet found freedom from oppression or from material want.

In some lands this fear has to do with the tribal structure, where the top chief is the big boss. I encountered this in some spots in Africa, where it became clear that in dealing with employees the top manager indeed has to look and act like an authoritarian boss. Although the natural tendency of Americans today is to move to open management styles—those involving all the employees—in other places this may sometimes be inappropriate. I consider this both a sensitive and a debatable issue, and still try to treat all people with respect and avoid being autocratic. Nevertheless, I do want to point out that people who have spent a lifetime in societies where most employees and customers come from tribal backgrounds and are not well educated, strongly believe that the boss has to appear indeed as a *boss.* They have pointed this out to me on more than one occasion. I suggest you assess the particular situation if you are in such a country.

STANDARD OF LIVING

Everyone seeks food, clothing, shelter, and security, but in varied ways; the need is universal, but this can also be one of the areas of greatest difference among nations. Some countries provide precious little of such basics.

All people in the world would no doubt like to provide a better life for their family and themselves. There is nevertheless an incredible disparity in standard of living between the countries of the world. In countries such as the U.S., Japan, and France, gross national product per person is more than $20,000 per year. Only twenty-five of the world's countries have per-capita GNP figures greater than $10,000 per year. In countries such as China, Zaire, and many more, it is less than $500 per person. In fact, the figure is less than $500 for more than half of the world's population.[1] Pretty surprising, isn't it? One wonders why the rest of the world didn't rise up long ago to get "their share." I think they just haven't known the extent of the disparity. I also think most of them will be pressing for more from now on.

RESPECT

Common to people throughout the world is the desire for respect. Each human being craves to have his existence recognized. Americans have such a strong belief in the individual they may find it difficult to understand that in many societies lower classes of people are almost non-people. In such places members of the upper classes may at times appear to ignore the very existence of members of the lower groups. Although you may work with members of the upper classes and must be sensitive to local social norms, you must guard against falling into the same behavior pattern.

Respect for others will earn you respect and devotion. It is very simple, this respect. How would you want to be treated? How would you want your spouse or your children treated?

OUR VALUES VERSUS THEIR VALUES

There is no question that, in almost any country of the world, you will believe that the U.S. has more goods, is more advanced and modern, is more powerful, and that Americans also work better, harder, and more productively. Such opinions have become ingrained in our values system, but many other countries do not share them. They may see the need for essentials like food, but the concept of working nonstop to the exclusion of all else is not comprehensible to many peoples of the world. In the developing world—and especially in the more "primitive" societies—it is difficult to convince people that work takes precedence over all else in life. You might consider, as you deal with such people, that their values and priorities may have something to say to you, and that Americans are not all-knowing and infallible. A great benefit personally in all your international efforts is that you learn as well as those with whom you are involved. The truth is that you grow and become a citizen of the world as well as of the U.S.

CONCLUSION

The popular song about all of us being people of the world applies here, for it represents the truth of the matter. We were born in the great country of the United States, and for that reason we either have or understand all that is available here. In the great majority of the world's countries, however, people do not have this degree of material excess. Nevertheless, we can identify with them. Understanding people and their goals and concerns is crucial to operating successfully in their country. Such understanding does require a little time and the building of relationships, but I have found this to be one of the great personal benefits of being in business around the world.

4

How to Explore and Enter a Country

This is where the fun begins. How do you investigate and enter the country you believe is right for you? Putting aside sweeping observations about the changing international world, the great opportunities, and the cultural differences and similarities, now you have to do it. Here are a few essential steps.

Investigating a Country

If you or your company believes a particular country may be attractive for your business, several sources of information will help you determine if your initial feeling is justified. I do suggest a team approach if possible, involving among others an experienced businessperson, ideally with a marketing background, and someone with financial and legal insights.

You should make contact with as many groups as possible that offer valuable information and insights before undertaking a full-blown exploratory visit to the country. If the review reveals serious concerns, it is time to move on to another candidate.

The following are valuable source groups (the Appendix provides more details, including addresses and telephone numbers):

- The foreign embassy of the subject country should be visited. Embassies are in Washington, DC, although the larger countries have consulates in major U.S. cities. In each embassy some dignitary is responsible for the commercial and economic area. He or she may be called the commercial counsel, or the commercial attaché, the economics counselor, or something less formal. The embassy will be happy to put you in touch, and a telephone call will get this started.

- Contact with the relevant parts of the U.S. government is also recommended. This includes the State Department, Commerce, the Trade Information Center, and perhaps the Office of the United States Trade Representative (USTR). You can learn a lot by having someone meet with the desk officers for the country in question at State and Commerce.

- International trade or government organizations can be very helpful as they likely see their role as supporting business ties between the U.S. and the subject country. These organizations often have a business professional as the executive and speak your language. Examples are the Council of the Americas and the U.S.–ASEAN Council on Business and Technology. Also helpful may be contact with a branch in the U.S. of the country's own chamber of commerce, if there is one.

- Nearby universities may have professors teaching on the subject who might have useful experience or contacts, and may even be natives of the country. Business schools and schools of international affairs can be very helpful.

- If you know of other American firms operating in the country, you should try to speak to the executive in the U.S. who is responsible. If the other company is not in your industry, you will generally find such executives more than willing to share "war stories" and offer advice.

- Some countries such as Singapore actually have offices in the U.S. to encourage American business involvement. The embassies should be able to help in this regard. If the country does have such a group, they will be staffed with people eager to answer your questions and likely aware of some of your concerns.

- Other organizations that will have information are major international commercial or development banks, all discussed in some depth in Chapter 7. The commercial banks want your business and should willingly provide help. Be sure to seek help from the non-American banks as well. In some areas, the American banks are not as extensively represented as these. A few of the major commercial banks have their own country-specific business guidebooks, with a focus on legal and financial regulations. The international development banks, such as the World Bank, are excellent sources of information, contacts, and possible funding.

- Major accounting firms that operate with international companies also can provide valuable information. Some publish their own country-specific guidebooks dealing with business regulations.

- Contact with international humanitarian aid, or "relief," groups may also provide assistance, especially if the country of your interest is one in which these groups are likely to be operating. A conversation with a representative may provide useful insights and even lead to beneficial operational arrangements. For example, in such countries these organizations need local funds, which in the future you may be willing to provide in exchange for dollars received back in the U.S. This exchange is discussed in Chapter 6. Examples of such groups are World Vision, Save the Children, and CARE.

- Numerous technical books may provide up-to-date facts, such as area almanacs. A few minutes in the business and travel sections of a large bookstore is well spent. Numerous books have been written on doing business in Japan, and there are now a few out on China and Mexico. As the extraordinary importance of the growing international markets becomes more widely known, there will no doubt be a growing flood of such country-specific books.

- If your organization is fairly large, a check of personnel records may turn up someone from the subject country or nationality who is on your payroll and who may be a big help. This, surprisingly, is very likely. This person in turn may be able to lead you to other pertinent contacts in your local community.

Visiting the Country

If your company is still interested after going through the above steps, it is time for the exploratory visit. This is a serious business trip by the team designed to collect as much meaningful information as possible. At least one member should have sufficient diplomatic skills to carry out effective meetings with senior local leaders, for these will occur if you are serious. In developing countries in particular, the high level of government officials that may participate in business-entry discussions is usually shocking to Americans. In addition, for countries in which English is not the primary or the official language, the visiting team will need to have one member who can translate for the group. Ideally, one of the team members will have this skill. If not, you may be able to obtain guidance to acquiring a translator through the contacts listed in the previous section, especially through the foreign embassy or the State Department.

One of the most important things to be gathered in this exploratory visit is simply the basic impression team members have of the country. Don't ever discount the instincts of experienced businesspeople; in some places this may be the best information you get. You will of course have to consider any personal biases you know a team member may have. For example, anyone who is uncomfortable outside luxury hotels and fine restaurants may not be happy in much of the world.

Here are points not to be missed:

- If you are aware of people or organizations with whom you would like to meet, endeavor to arrange such meetings before leaving to assure that the trip is worthwhile. In small countries especially, key individuals are so stretched they may be in or out of the country with little advance warning. Cable, telephones, and faxes will become your standard mode of operation.

- Discuss the trip in advance with your contacts in the country's embassy to gain as much assistance as possible in setting up meetings. Embassy staff do not want you to be inconvenienced unnecessarily, nor do they want their country's business and government leaders embarrassed. They likely are interested in your trip being a success.

- Be certain to include visits with appropriate local government officials, especially in a smaller country, as in such places the officials are often crucial to business dealings. In developing countries you might wish to speak to officials in the central bank, the ministry of finance, the ministry of labor, and the ministry of trade or commerce, for example.

- Notify the State Department of your trip and ask it to contact the U.S. embassy in the country to set up a tentative meeting with the U.S. ambassador or commercial attaché. You might want to meet with the embassy more than once in the visit if you are to be in the country for a while. This is one way to check your observations confidentially with people who are supposed to be on your side. It's worth noting that there is a wide range of background among ambassadors and staffs. In recent years they have become more attuned to issues of commerce, but it is possible to find one who has little or no such interest.

- When in the country try to meet with a few top managers of local operations of American firms (or Canadian or Western European firms); if they are not in your industry they will usually be happy to offer insights. I would also strongly recommend a contact with the local branch of the American Chamber of Commerce. There are many of these around the world.

- Before the trip be sure to take care of details such as passports, visas, and inoculations. If you are going to many third-world countries, medical precautions are not to be taken lightly; these are discussed further in Chapter 13.

WHAT ARE YOU LOOKING FOR IN THESE INVESTIGATIONS?

Before visiting a country (and ideally before beginning any research), it is highly advisable to establish selection criteria. If you are searching for an area in which to build a large, technically advanced manufacturing facility, you can quickly screen out many sites. Countries that don't have the skilled people to operate such a plant and will not allow you to bring in your staff can be disqualified, unless you want to offer an extensive training program in return for financial breaks, such as exemption from taxes for ten years.

If you want a market that looks as much like the U.S. as possible, you will be considering Canada, Britain, Australia, New Zealand, France, and Germany. If you can just be a tiny bit more adventurous, you can look into Asian countries that, although admittedly different, have strong capitalist drives and higher growth prospects, such as Singapore, Malaysia, and Thailand.

Perhaps you are looking for long-term growth markets and are not so interested in immediate returns. If you are this farsighted (as are many Japanese and European companies), then the newly awakening lands might be just right for you. It will be difficult to get your business started, but once you are there and have a secure spot, you will be able to grow with the market. Mexico, China, and Argentina fit this mold, and with perhaps a longer-term outlook, India, Poland, Hungary, the Czech Republic, Ghana, and Zimbabwe are candidates.

To reword the old cliché, what appears to one person a candidate to avoid at all costs may seem to another a paradise of opportunity. It all has to do with your particular business, your goals, your ability to take risks, your vision, and your available time frame.

Within this overview, there are a few qualities that you clearly should seek. Most countries will not be able to meet all these to your satisfaction, so your decision becomes something of a trade-off. Specifically, you should look for these attributes, all discussed in other chapters in the book:

- a stable government
- a positive government attitude toward private business enterprise
- reassuring investment policies and laws, such as the right to repatriate dividends to the home country
- a strong financial structure, one that will provide sufficient availability of convertible currency acceptable in world markets to support your business efforts
- availability of sufficient skilled labor
- the right to bring in expert talent as needed
- access to participation in the local market
- attractive tax and investment benefits to an entering company
- a marketplace not overflowing with competitors
- a market with significant growth potential

Many more attributes are desirable, but these are essential.

To What Extent Do You Want To Be Involved?

Throughout the investigation, the desired extent of company involvement in the country should be in the considerations of all involved. This question most likely cannot be answered without conducting the investigations and learning firsthand the specific issues to be faced.

Here are six basic ways you might enter, listed in order of increasing involvement in the country:

1. The method of least involvement is to sell products made offshore to customers in the country who pay at receipt. In other words, you just take orders in the United States and ship them off. You will need someone on your staff who understands how to ship internationally and who understands basic financial documents such as the letter of credit (see Chapter 5), but not much more.

2. Only slightly advanced from point 1 is having a local representative, or agent, in the country who attempts to sell your product by calling on potential customers. There is almost no investment on your part. You just have to locate such a representative, and it is beneficial if that person has established business contacts and a solid marketing network.

3. The next-higher level of involvement entails having a distributor in the country. In so doing you are really formally represented, although it is not your operation. Rather than selling to customers, you sell in to the distributor, who takes it from there. He is more than just a representative who takes orders. He has a company that sells, markets, advertises, distributes, and supports your product. Obviously, you will have to develop this relationship and provide appropriate support to the distributor.

4. Next, you may decide to set up your own business, but not feeling confident enough of the market, you take a local partner. This partner should have knowledge of the market, and contacts with banks, marketing channels, and the government as necessary. You bring the product and the know-how. This

partner should be someone you can trust and who can produce.

5. A deeper involvement is to operate the business without a partner but to take a local shareholder or two. Local shareholders will ideally provide funds and contacts that your business needs. They may not be involved in the running of the business, but if they are influential, they may someday wield that influence, especially in the smaller countries.

6. Finally, you may set up a subsidiary with no local ownership. In many countries this is impossible, as partial local ownership is required; nevertheless, your business may be so interesting and important that it can obtain permission to operate as a completely foreign-owned subsidiary. Of course, if there is no local ownership, there may be less local government interest in resolving your problems. Without local involvement in ownership, your operation will also have less insider knowledge of and contact with the local business and government community and the local culture.

These seem to me the basic alternatives. There may be more, but others should be a variation on the above.

In all but perhaps points 1 and 6 you will notice the great dependence on local individuals of influence and business knowledge. I would maintain that in point 6 you had better have such people on the payroll, unless your business is simple indeed and very small-scale.

Governments prefer that you make meaningful investments, not just minor amounts that are then leveraged in local funds up to the needed amount. The methods in points 1, 2, and 3 therefore are not going to be as well received as the other three. This is one local view probably always opposed to your instincts and perhaps to your best interests. Quite naturally, governments are looking for employment opportunities for their citizens and a commitment to the country that an investment in a plant or other significant facility represents.

Of course, you are not locked into one form of operation forever. Entering often is evolutionary, beginning first with local representation such as in point 1 or 2 above, moving later through the distributor phase, and finally arriving at a full-blown subsidiary operation as the business grows and prospers. The possibility of such evolution might even be indicated in your early negotiations with governmental authorities, but you should be careful not to promise too much, as they may be endlessly pressing you for such action once your initial operation has begun.

(If your company is very small, with perhaps just a handful of employees, your options for participating in the international business world are more limited than are those of larger companies. Your options in this case are primarily those in points 1 and 2. If your company is this small, in addition to reading the chapters of this book, you should also read Section VIII of the Appendix. There a step-by-step guide is specifically designed for use by the smallest businesses in evaluating and getting involved in the international market.)

Choosing the Local "Partner"

This becomes crucial in many entry plans. Whether he or she is a real equity partner, a distributor, a shareholder, or a representative, this person is nevertheless a vital cog in your business efforts. Where do you find such a person?

The search should begin while your team is in the country doing its exploratory work. Many of the sources are those noted already. Local branches of international banks you trust may have some suggestions for you, especially as to local shareholders. Also, the local U.S. embassy may be able to steer you in some direction. Other sources of suggestions may be the top managers of local operations of foreign companies, American or otherwise. The local branch of the American Chamber of Commerce is a good source. As in the U.S., one contact will lead to another. If you are so fortunate as to be in an industry with an association that can make recommendations for the country, so much the better. Depending on the size of the firm, your outside lawyer or law firm back home may be able to recommend someone in the country for your consideration.

As individuals or local companies are identified and you begin to make contact, there are some elements not to ignore:

- Be alert for the political connections of the person or company. Such connections may be beneficial in getting your operation going but may be disastrous if you and this individual or company have a serious disagreement. He has the government on his side. In many of the smaller developing countries, this is a lot of clout and may include the regulatory authorities and the courts. (Even if the local courts are objective, a dispute between a local citizen or company and a person or company from another nation will have an unavoidable local bias.)

    Many years ago in the Middle East, I was at a dinner at a home of a distant member of the ruling family. In the course of the evening, he drifted into conversation about dealing with unscrupulous people, or, I gathered, anyone with whom he did not agree. He went on to boast that by placing a telephone call he could stop anyone from leaving the country. He could indeed seal the airports and borders to stop someone whom he felt was treating him unfairly. I of course wondered if he told this story for my benefit.

One other serious concern with the political connections of the partner is that the current government may lose in the next election (or the next coup, depending on the local environment). In that case, your venture would be connected with an individual or company out of favor with the ruling government. A far better course for a foreign-owned business is to steer clear of any obvious ties to a government or to any particular politician or official.

- In any negotiations with the prospective partner, do not give away control of your operation. No business deal is worth the headaches that come from such an arrangement.

- Be sure to structure the initial relationship and any written agreement so that you have an escape clause and can get out if you discover the Titanic under your feet. These are not difficult to set up. The most drastic are simply to state that at certain times, such as after six months or a year, either party can cancel the venture, perhaps with some money changing hands. The goal is to negotiate the best such provision for your company, which in this case includes setting minimal escape costs for you. Ideally, you would like the only right to escape, but you also hope to hold the partner in the deal and likely will have to give some escape rights to him as well.

- Perhaps most distressful, there will always be local individuals who sound great but who in practice bring much less to the venture than anticipated. This is a serious concern, and despite all your investigation, it is one you cannot entirely avoid. Sometimes there is no way of knowing without trying, then hoping that the cost of stubbing your toe will not be too great. The escape clause noted above comes in very handy in such situations.

- One last caution. The partner will have local contacts and will know the local problems of doing business—how difficult or how easy something is. You
  will be at his mercy for quite a while; he knows that,
  of course.

LOCAL COUNSEL

From the moment you decide you are serious about the
country, you should seek expert local counsel. This will
probably come from a lawyer, but not always. Most important, it should come from someone or some organization
that not only can interpret the local rules and policies but
also knows how the powers that be view them. This advisor
knows how to get things done, the hurdles you must get
over, and is trustworthy. You find such a person much the
same way that you find your partner, but this should be
done earlier and it is probably easier. The U.S. embassy
should have some suggestions, as well as managers of local
subsidiaries of foreign companies, and certainly the local
American Chamber of Commerce, if there is one. Especially for this position, your outside counsel back home
may be able to recommend someone or at least a starting
place for beginning the search. As noted before, however,
this counsel is not necessarily a lawyer but is, much more
importantly, someone "in the know" in the country.

If this counsel does not have all the needed skill
areas, you will surely also need advice from local tax and
finance experts who understand the banking and financial picture in the country. This may be someone from the
local branch of an international bank.

NEGOTIATING WITH GOVERNMENT

This is an especially important part of entering a foreign land, and negotiations with officials are likely to be more extensive—and different—than you anticipate if your background is solely in the U.S. Chapters 11 and 12 specifically focus on governmental involvement in your efforts, and Chapter 15 provides advice on this aspect of negotiations.

CONCLUSION

In your investigation in the country, don't forget the points raised in other chapters of this book. For example, review with the local central bank or other appropriate authority the rules for remission of dividends; check into policies that affect your freedom to bring in your own managers; look into local living conditions for such employees, and much more.

Ask all the questions at the outset. You won't get a second chance.

5

FUNNY MONEY

Remember, as a kid, saving bottle caps: Coke, Pepsi, or Nehi? If you didn't, I'll bet you had a friend who did. Bottle caps were a readily available collection. The hobby may be going out of style today with the new plastic bottle tops, but it wasn't too many years ago that it was still popular.

If you or a friend had a collection like that, you could use it to play games. One thing I used it for was money. My sister and I often would play cards; we didn't have money to bet, so we played for bottle caps. When the game was over, one of us might have several more bottle caps than the other. That would feel really good for a while, but eventually the winner would just throw them back into the shoe box with the rest of the bottle caps. After all, they had no value except in one of our games. Winning looked good for a while, but only for awhile.

Some countries operate with currency that is much like bottle caps. They call it metecais, cruzeiros, pesos, zaires, rubles, or zlotys, for example.

If you choose to operate in such a country, remember that the currency has no value elsewhere.

If your business venture involves France, Germany, Singapore, Hong Kong, Britain, or similar spots, you do not have this concern. Those countries have currencies readily acceptable (and convertible) on the world stage. They are in fact termed "convertible" currencies, or more popularly, "hard" currencies. It is easy to exchange German marks for U.S. dollars, British pounds, French francs, and so forth. There are of course exchange rates, but those are well understood and reported in the *Wall Street Journal* and other daily newspapers. The economies of these countries are so sound that their currencies are valued throughout the world.

Hard currencies are a sight better than the bottle-cap currencies of many countries, which are not readily convertible into hard currencies and which quite naturally are often referred to as "soft" currencies. Such money is acceptable only within its country's own borders. You cannot exchange any meaningful amount of zaires outside the country of Zaire. If you are going to do business there and somehow you manage to negotiate so that you can repatriate dividends to the United States, you will have to find a way in Zaire to exchange the zaires earned there for U.S. dollars, or at least for some hard currency that you can eventually convert to U.S. dollars.

This is neither a minor point nor a minor problem. Many more countries have soft currencies than hard ones. You very likely will want to do business with some of them because many are where the growth is going to be. If you are going to be involved with the soft-currency countries, you must structure your operations, your deals, and your relationships so that you allow for this very significant issue.

Complicating matters, there are some countries where you may find customers not using even bottle caps. They may want to give you shoes, oil, or who knows what else.

Barter is still alive and well in some places, especially the newly freed lands of Eastern Europe and the former Soviet Union. There are companies that do very well in this type of deal. The skills needed are not your usual daily operating talents. This is think-on-your-feet, take-a-risk, guess-the-market, how-well-can-you-cover-yourself business. Some companies are excellent at this. Anyone who likes to get out and *deal* will like this environment. Most corporate bureaucrats are terrified of this type of business, but it is real.

What are the strategies to be followed in dealing with countries with such strange currency concerns? Fortunately, the difficulties are not too great, but they are unique and are not encountered by the majority of American business people. Like other business problems, they are just something different, something to be mastered.

Soft Currency Strategies

Use Local Currency to Buy Needed Material for Local Use

A primary concern if you are in business in a soft-currency country is that you may have difficulty exchanging local currency for hard currency—for example, to buy needed materials from outside the country, to send dividend payments home, or to take your investment out of the country should you decide to close or sell the local operation. In a soft-currency country, demand for hard currency by businesses and citizens probably exceeds the available supply.

This is not as easy as it looks. Suppliers from outside the country will want to be paid in U.S. dollars, British pounds, or some other hard currency, not in bottle caps.

In your entry negotiations, try to cover with the local central bank the possibility of obtaining "guarantees" for hard-currency availability for purchase of raw material. Also, investigate with the major international development banks their possible guaranteed supply of hard currency for material purchase.

Pay Local Expenses in the Soft Currency

Absolutely. You do not want to increase your problem by paying out hard currency locally. This may seem an unrealistic concern, but the local government as well as your local employees may see you and your organization as a potential source of hard currency.

Borrow in Soft Currency for Local Financial Needs

If the operation needs to borrow funds for local use, there are usually benefits to borrowing local currency from local banks if possible.

First, any soft-currency country is likely to have internal inflation. When you make loan payments in the future, you will be paying back amounts in local currency that are worth significantly less as a result. For example, suppose you borrow 1,000 ducats and today each ducat will buy a bag of cement. Suppose further that the annual inflation rate is 100 percent, which is low for some soft-currency countries. In just a year, for example, a bag of cement will cost two ducats. When you make a loan repayment in a year, each ducat you will be repaying the bank is worth in real terms half what it was when you borrowed it.

A second benefit is that your local debt will tie directly to the local economy. Very likely the value of any hard currency brought into the country will greatly escalate over the years in relation to the value of the local currency. If one U.S. dollar brought in today is worth two ducats, in a year it will be worth four. Therefore, in repaying the debt in the future, you always have the option of bringing in a smaller amount of dollars than would be needed today to provide the loan amount. Also, in translating your local books to dollar accounting for the parent company, the local debt becomes much less significant over time.

In addition to these benefits, by borrowing locally in local soft currency your company will avoid bringing into the country additional hard currency, something you may not want to do, as discussed later in this section and in Chapter 6.

A possible counterbalance to these benefits is the interest rate charged by the local banks on the loan. This rate may be so high that it negates your projection of the inflation and devaluation benefits noted above plus the nonquantifiable benefit of avoiding bringing in hard currency. Certainly, you (or whoever is responsible for making the borrowing decision) must consider this trade-off. Even if the local interest rate is so large as to offset the projected inflation and devaluation benefits, you may still choose to borrow locally rather than bring in hard currency that may be difficult to recover later.

In the case of hard-currency borrowing for the local operation, the debt on the parent company's books remains constant. When translated into local currency, moreover, it becomes greater on the local books over time, as the local currency decreases in value versus the hard currency that must be repaid.

Sell As Much As Possible in Hard Currency

This is a real winner. If you can be involved in making a product that is marketable outside the country's borders, you have a great advantage. Selling for hard currency eases your funny-money problem and also wins you friends with the country's government. Of course, once those hard-currency funds are received by your operation in the country, they will be converted by the local banks to soft currency. If you indeed plan to market outside the country's borders, negotiate ahead with the government and its central bank to ensure that your operation will be allowed to claim a significant portion of that hard currency for use in purchasing raw material from outside the country. You should also try to negotiate the right to leave a portion of the hard currency from sales in an international bank. Perhaps you might negotiate the right to use some for payment of your annual dividend.

Minimize Any Hard-Currency Amounts Brought into the Country

You do not want to bring in a huge hard-currency investment to start up your business. Such an action immediately converts funds that are relatively stable in value and acceptable throughout the world into soft-currency funds that are more volatile and are likely acceptable only in the host country. Furthermore, as noted earlier, in a soft-currency country, there is always the question of whether there will be sufficient hard currency available in the country for you to exchange local currency and move this investment should you desire to do so. Certainly you will have to bring in some funds, but in all negotiations with the local government and the banks you should seek to minimize hard currency that comes in and is immediately part of the capital base of the local operation.

One possibility here is to attempt to start up the local operation on a shoestring, with minimal capital. You would then bring in just enough capital to qualify to borrow in local currency from a local bank.

Another approach is to negotiate with the local government so that the amount of hard currency you bring in gives you at least a guaranteed amount of hard-currency availability for exchange of your locally earned currency, so that you have a base to count on for dividend submission or for purchasing materials from outside.

One more option is to find a company already in the country that might have a large amount of local currency. It is sometimes possible to work out a deal whereby you pay that firm in hard currency offshore and receive in the country local currency of a larger amount than you would have received at the official exchange rate. This may sound suspicious, but it is possible, and you may be able to work it out with the involvement of the local central bank. After all, the country probably wants you to come.

There are also the various international banks, especially development banks such as the World Bank, the African Development Bank, the Asian Development Bank, and more, all reviewed in Chapter 7. They may be able to help minimize hard-currency imports, although they are more helpful in financing.

Last, and very possible, is the option of bringing in machinery, equipment, inventory, and anything else needed from your existing stocks and reaching an agreed valuation to count as your capital investment in the company. The benefit of this is that the local capital valuation may in fact be higher than the real material value to you elsewhere in the world. This would be the case especially if the local operation is not to be as technically advanced as some in the most industrialized countries and you are able to move in materials no longer of significant value elsewhere.

The Ideal

In a soft-currency country, the ideal business, then, utilizes local labor and materials, all of which can be paid for with local currency, and results in products sold outside the country for hard currency. Such a venture will probably lead you to a position of importance in the country; indeed, you may move there to live in regal splendor.

The converse of this rosy scenario is the true disaster, that of buying materials in hard currency, paying some expenses and borrowing in hard currency, and selling the finished products in soft currency. If this is your plan, you are likely to lose your shirt, for you will bring upon yourself the opposite of the strategic results just described.

If your business involves only sales to the country but no physical operations there, the ideal situation is to collect for any sales in hard currency at the time the product is delivered. A safe instrument for this is the irrevocable, confirmed letter of credit described later in this chapter.

HARD-CURRENCY STRATEGIES

You probably thought you were out of the woods if you were in a hard-currency country; not so. Yes, you can exchange that currency for good old U.S. dollars; but suppose that you bring in raw materials for which you pay ten U.S. dollars, and the exchange rate to the local currency is 1:1. You spend ten ducats in local currency, which translates to ten dollars and buys the material. Now suppose that you use this material to make your product, and you sell it for fifteen ducats. A tidy sum; good work. The sales manager gets a pat on the back. You ask the purchasing manager to buy the same amount of raw material again. He investigates and comes back with disturbing news: It seems the ducat is now worth only half a U.S. dollar, so the fifteen ducats you received for your product will convert to only seven dollars and fifty cents. You actually lost money in U.S. dollars.

Amazing, isn't it? The local manager shows on his books a tidy profit for the month. The executive back at the U.S. headquarters reports a loss in his "dollar" accounting. Is something fishy?

Indeed. The real-world problem in dealings between nations with hard currencies likely will not be of this magnitude, but it is real. Just watch the exchange rate between the U.S. dollar and the British pound vary over a month. You can check daily in most major newspapers.

What do you do? For basically stable exchange rates, you probably just try to manage your business so that the rate fluctuation is not large enough to render a disastrous result. If there are risks of significant swings in the rate, you will want to consider hedging your expected revenues; that is, protecting yourself against future dramatic exchange rate swings. For peace of mind, you cover future uncertainties by selling the local currency forward to lock in a U.S. dollar exchange rate. Thus, if the local currency drops greatly in value versus the dollar, you are covered by the much-stronger exchange rate you have already purchased. This protects you from earning a great deal in ducats but finding the profit translated to nothing in dollars due to a sudden drop in exchange value of the ducat. This costs you something, of course, but not much compared to the potential problem if a swing in exchange rates is anticipated.

Let's look at an example. Suppose in this foreign country your business is doing well, and you would like to send a dividend back to the U.S. in two months. In the fiscal year just completed your business has earned income to support a dividend payment of 20,000 ducats. Unfortunately, the local currency has been fluctuating in its exchange rate with the dollar, and you are fearful that the earnings expressed in local currency may be worth less in dollars in two months than they are today. Currently, two ducats may be exchanged for one U.S. dollar, so you hope to be able to send the home office a dividend of $10,000. You ask your treasurer to "fix" this two-for-one exchange rate for the future dividend transmission. The treasurer then goes into the financial market and secures this current exchange rate for your dividend transmission in the future. The treasurer literally buys the right to exchange 20,000 ducats into $10,000 U.S. in two months, regardless of what the actual exchange rate for the ducat is at that future date. This is a very real problem, and it occurs in spots like Australia and New Zealand, not just in developing countries.

This is why you pay international treasurers and international bankers. That's their job, and you need to consult them.

For some soft-currency countries this is not a problem, as the exchange rate is fixed by the government and may not vary for years. There may unfortunately be few dollars available to make exchanges at that official rate. A few soft-currency countries have this fluctuating-rate problem in spades; Brazil and Peru are a couple of good examples. They are frequently repairing their exchange rates and embarking on new courses; then suddenly the rate will change so fast the ink can't dry before a new rate must be set. This is when your financial manager, your purchasing manager, and your accountants in the local operation and in your headquarters earn their stripes. They won't be sitting back adding up columns of figures at month's end; they will be following rates hourly, buying or selling currency, timing purchases of needed materials. If you operate where the rate does fluctuate wildly, a treasurer with currency-management skills is essential.

BARTER

There's not much to say about this; the subject says it all. As already mentioned, some nations have no way of paying for goods or services, and they or their companies may offer you other goods instead. Former Soviet Union nations and Eastern European countries engage in this. Serious questions must be asked:

Can the Value of the Goods
Be Realistically Estimated?

This is not easy to answer. Remember, not only are you likely being offered goods from an industry in which you do not have expertise, but also you are being offered these goods far from any market. Unless these goods are within your company's area of knowledge, before making any deal you should immediately secure the services of a trader company. These firms survive by dealing around the world in goods rather than cash. They can estimate value for you and even offer to dispose of the goods for a fee.

Can the Quality of the Goods Be Controlled?

You should negotiate the right to have your designated experts inspect the goods at critical points in the process. Don't wait to check on the goods until after you have provided your merchandise or service.

Will the Goods Be Accepted
into Potential Markets?

The trader should be able to help here. Certainly items from struggling countries that must engage in barter may not meet the import standards of many countries. A good international import/export lawyer is a plus.

LETTER OF CREDIT

If your business consists only of selling merchandise into countries, your currency problems are readily handled.

For sales into a soft currency country or to a high credit-risk customer anywhere, sell using a letter of credit. The problems of hard-currency availability and collectibility are dealt with by the customer and the international banks. You just sit tight and wait for the customer to arrive at a successful letter with his bank, which in turn works with a major international bank you trust, and that has offices in the U.S. Upon notification that the letter is arranged (that is, that your money is ready), you ship to the customer. Notification should come from the international bank, not from the customer (who may be only too eager to make this statement) nor his bank. The confirmation should include acknowledgment that the letter of credit is irrevocable.

Requiring a letter of credit may limit the number of potential customers, but it is about as safe as you can get. When a customer sets up this letter, in the end it is the international bank saying to you that your money is available. The customer of course has to satisfy the banking requirements, which probably means he has great credit in his home country or has deposited the sum required with his bank, which has in turn found the necessary hard currency.

In truly desperate countries it may be impossible to obtain a letter of credit simply because no one can arrange to get any hard currency. You just won't sell there, unless you like bottle caps.

RUNAWAY INFLATION

You may encounter one other unique currency difficulty. Some nations, generally the truly developing ones, have extraordinary internal inflation rates. Brazil is probably the best example of this. Rates there in past years have been in the neighborhood of 30 percent inflation per month. In mid-1993 inflation was again at that level.

This is not something most U.S. business people have encountered.

I recall an instance several years ago when an executive from Brazil came to the U.S. to get advice from pension experts. After a day of meetings in which he described his problems, he was told by the U.S. experts that there just was no such thing as an inflation rate as high as 30 percent per month. They simply did not believe him! (Not all American business people are so naive or uninformed, but this does illustrate the challenge facing American business executives as they seek overseas markets.)

The additional concern for you, beyond those already expressed, is that your financial managers in a country with such a high inflation rate must be astute and flexible in adjusting all prices, costs, and wages to respond quickly. A frequent practice is to have employee wages updated often. This is where indexing comes in. You may have heard about this; it's a horrible practice that of course fuels the overall inflation rate. Nevertheless, your operation must survive; it must have realistic prices to recover steadily escalating costs and be able to buy new materials at rising prices. Furthermore, employees must receive a livable wage.

Such wild inflation is not typical of many nations, but it does occur and will require special management skill in the local operation, as well as understanding in the home office by those responsible for the foreign operation.

ALL THAT GLITTERS IS NOT GOLD

This statement pretty much sums up this chapter. Much of the world's currency is funny money. It's a whole new collection of concerns.

6

CAN YOU GET YOUR MONEY OUT?

If you operate successfully in a foreign country and earn an attractive profit but cannot get any of it out of the country, have you accomplished anything? After all you did invest to expand your business, to earn income, and to increase your sales and market value; what was this effort worth?

The answer can be very little. Perhaps if you have a tolerant auditor you will be able to include your performance in that country in your consolidated income statement, but don't count on it. Furthermore, it has probably taken a lot of effort by some of your company's most talented people to make this operation successful. Even the word "successful" doesn't seem to fit now, does it?

A related question should also be firmly implanted in your decision-making consciousness as you consider setting up operations in another country. If the operation does not go well and you choose to pull out by

selling the operation or closing it down, will it be possible
to repatriate the original investment? ("Repatriate" is popular international business jargon that refers to bringing
something back home; e.g., bringing back to the U.S. a
share of the profits made offshore, or the original investment, or even an employee and his family who have
been in a foreign land. In the financial area, people
sometimes refer to repatriating capital as "liberating" an
investment.)

These are serious issues and should be answered positively before you begin establishing operations in a country. Certainly, the modern industrial nations of the West
are generally open on these points, although you will need
to investigate thoroughly local dividend and tax regulations. For many of the world's poorer or developing countries, however, these are real concerns. Let's look at the
key components.

DOES THE GOVERNMENT RESTRICT DIVIDEND REMISSION?

Regardless of any other factors, this is a clear indicator of
the government's posture toward private enterprise and of
how easy a future business relationship will be. The local
counsel recommended earlier should apprise you of all
local regulations regarding repatriation of dividends and
other related matters. This advisor should provide practical interpretation of what is really likely to happen in
addition to reporting the rules on the books.

Some nations restrict the profit that can be remitted
by having a percentage standard, such as 50 percent of the
profit earned, or perhaps 15 percent of the invested capital. You need to know this early.

Is Hard Currency Available to Remit Dividends?

Even if the country permits your operation to remit dividends home, this may be merely a moral victory if there are no hard-currency funds available from the country's central bank to use. This problem is serious throughout Africa, in parts of Asia/Pac Rim, in areas of Latin America, in the newly freed nations of Eastern Europe, and in the former Soviet republics. Most of the world's countries have soft currency, and you will find that hard-currency availability for dividend remission is a genuine concern. You should discuss the issue with the central bank and other relevant financial authorities during your entry investigations. It's better to learn at the outset if there is a stumbling block to such an obvious business objective.

What About Possible Disputes with Your Local Partner(s)?

If you have local shareholders or partners in your operation, there is always the chance that they may not want to pay out dividends, preferring to plow all funds back into the business. More likely, especially in a poor country and if a government-owned company is your partner, there is a chance your local shareholders or partners will want to receive maximum dividends. This creates an especially unattractive situation if you must pay out large dividends to keep them happy but cannot repatriate your share, leaving it to languish in a local bank in local currency, where it is likely to lose real value daily due to both the high rate of local inflation and the decreasing relative value of the local currency to hard currency (i.e., its devaluation).

A point to keep in mind is that local partners or shareholders may in some countries have considerable influence with the government and central bank. You may not always be as free to act as you would like.

POLITICAL REALITY CHECK

This is a good item to have on any checklist as you consider entering a country. Regardless of the formal regulations, consider the likelihood that repatriating income will not be appreciated by the local government. Especially in poorer developing countries, this can become a problem as the government is forced to listen to your repeated petition for hard currency to send home. In the eyes of most local governments, all American companies are rich and full of funds anyway.

REPATRIATION OF INVESTMENT WHEN BUSINESS ENDS

This is a related issue but includes the area of investment guidelines. Each country has some, and your local counsel should inform you of them. You can always get information from the local U.S. embassy, or from the host country's embassy in the United States, but it is highly recommended to have the (ideally) impartial advice of a counselor knowledgeable in the local situation.

Repatriating your original capital is not at the top of your list when you are setting up an operation, but it should not be ignored. Not every venture can be a success, and your ability to recover part or all of your original capital will reduce the cost of any failure and encourage you and your company to try again.

Blocked Cash—Concerns and Strategies

Anyone engaged in international business recoils at the mention of the term "blocked cash," funds that for any of several possible reasons you are unable to repatriate from a foreign operation to your home office in the U.S. It nevertheless becomes an issue at times, despite all the expert advice and the best efforts of your employees (and even, perhaps, despite the good intentions of the local authorities).

Blocked cash problems most likely will arise if you are operating in a country that finds itself with insufficient hard currency to cover all its foreign financial obligations. If this occurs, you can bet you will have difficulty obtaining all your needs, and if your local operation is successful and is earning income, your cash balances in local currency will begin to grow.

Other possible causes of blocked cash relate to the laws of the land; specifically, restrictions on repatriation of dividends or capital, or perhaps even limitations on the amount of income that can be declared as dividends, regardless of the repatriation issue. Whatever the cause, you will find this situation unique the first time you encounter it. Just what do you do with cash that you wanted to repatriate to the shareholders back home?

It's unpleasant to consider. All you can really do is minimize the impact of a bad situation. Fundamentally, you will want to preserve the real value of that cash. If you are in a soft-currency country (as would likely be the case), and/or if you are in a country whose currency depreciates versus the dollar on a steady basis, you have to do something. In addition, if your host country has high local inflation, you may have to take bold action just to protect the real value of the currency that you hold. Brazil comes to mind as an example of this, as do Peru, Russia, and many African countries.

In almost all instances, you do not want to leave your blocked cash in a local bank. Most likely, the interest earned there will not be sufficient to preserve its real value. In fact, in some places banks may pay no interest; strict observance of Sharia (Islamic) law in parts of the Middle East dictates this practice, for example. You have several options to avoid such an imbroglio.

Invest in Needed Improvements or Maintenance to Your Operation

This is perhaps the best step if you truly need such improvements. It will ideally enable you to repatriate future earnings if the situation improves in the country rather than use them for local investment, as that will now have been done. Further, these improvements should make your operation more competitive and more profitable, thereby producing more future dividends for remission.

Real Estate

There is only so much investment you can intelligently make in your local operation. What do you do with the rest?

A time-honored use of blocked cash is to invest in something that will not depreciate in value in relation to either local or world currencies. The most readily available item is real estate. Some firms even get involved in building offices or apartment buildings with blocked cash, or in developing housing. This is better than it appears at first glance. In some developing countries, it is possible to structure such deals so that renters are foreign government embassies or consulates, or are branches of foreign companies, all of whom pay rent in hard currency. You may be able to set all this up with the central bank in advance so that you can use this hard currency in exchange for future local profits for remission as dividends.

Provide Financing to Local Exporters

It is at times possible to use your blocked cash to help finance another local business and in the process actually get some hard cash offshore; an agricultural effort is an example. Perhaps a local coffee plantation needs local funds to package and market its product; you can provide the funds in return for the right to use part of the hard-currency receipts gained by the plantation on its export sales.

Exchange with International Agency or Company

It may be that an international agency or company is setting up operations in the country and needs local currency. You may be able to negotiate supplying that organization's local-currency needs in exchange for hard currency paid by that organization to your parent company offshore. Of course, the organization will expect a discount on the exchange since it is helping you out, but you will likely be willing to grant it. This is not as far-fetched as it appears, should be reviewed with local central banks, and is all aboveboard if you keep everyone informed and obtain concurrence. Major international companies and relief organizations may be interested in such an arrangement.

Investment in Another Enterprise

This is a decision to be made only in a long-term planning perspective. It implies that you will be in the country a long time.

The idea is to invest in a local business that generates hard currency, such as a mine whose ore is sold outside the country for hard currency—copper mine, gold mine, or coal mine, for example. The government will appreciate expanding a hard-currency generating operation, and you should be able to negotiate the rights to a portion of the hard currency in return for your making a significant investment in local funds.

You should of course avoid entering a business of which you have no knowledge, or one that will drain management talent from your main operations. Investing local currency in an ongoing, well-run company to enable increased production is probably the best approach.

This active investment (and thus ownership) position is different than the earlier suggestion of simply providing financing to a local company that needs funds to take its products to market; the investment approach is a long-term commitment.

CONCLUSION

A bird in the hand is worth two in the bush. Remember, if your local operation indeed has blocked cash that it is having difficulty remitting to the home office, it at least has the blocked cash. There is always the hope that someday—and perhaps that day is just a few weeks or months away—the country's central bank will have sufficient hard currency for your remission, or perhaps the local government will relax its policy restricting such dividends. If you enter into an elaborate scheme that ties up that blocked cash for years in some other project, you may not have those funds available when this opportunity comes. Even worse, some of the schemes to utilize your blocked cash may use it up forever.

Certainly you should investigate all realistic alternatives for getting your money out, and those described in this chapter do indeed work at times. Just be cautious of schemes that promise too much.

The best advice is never to get into a blocked cash situation, and the best means to that end is a thorough investigation with the local central bank and other authorities during your exploration phase of how likely this is to become a problem.

7

How to Finance

It takes money to get something going. No doubt you are apprehensive about putting your funds into the host country, and you will use every effort to minimize the hard currency you bring in. Even so, you will need money, if not hard currency then soft local currency. A visit to the banks with which you have long been doing business may be discouraging. Except for a few giant international banks in the U.S., most may not feel comfortable about lending you funds to take offshore, especially to developing countries. If you are apprehensive about taking your money offshore, imagine how your banker feels. So where do you turn?

There are numerous sources of funds, and we will explore them here. These sources include:

- International commercial banks
- Banks in the host country
- Development banks

- AID programs
- The U.S. government
- Local government
- Partners
- Other sources

We will look into not only these sources but also some avenues of unique protection for your investment, political risk insurance if you are considering especially unstable areas of the world.

INTERNATIONAL COMMERCIAL BANKS

These institutions are not just a potential source of funds; they are also very good suppliers of information. As you explore these, you will likely encounter someone who has worked with your host country and may have reams of experiences to relate. The American banks are by no means the only leaders in this area. Certainly you should contact them, the most obvious being Citibank.

Also promising are the European banks, such as Barclays of Britain, which has offices throughout the world and is a fount of information and consultation. Barclays has offices in the U.S. and will provide material on various countries. Another international bank of great clout and insight is Deutsche Bank, which has a global network and has expertise in Eastern Europe and the former Soviet republics. If you own or work for a big international company already, you may easily discuss your plans with many other international banks in foreign lands such as Switzerland, but it will be far easier for most companies to pursue their interests through offices of these banks in the U.S.

LOCAL BANKS IN THE COUNTRY

In sophisticated countries, banking will not be difficult. You can work with leading local banks and also contact branches of the major international banks. In less developed countries, your only local contact may be a national bank—perhaps the government's central bank itself—although there may be a branch of a major international bank, and perhaps other opportunities. In such areas, you will probably contact the local bank to borrow in local currency. This is usually good practice, especially if this currency is highly unstable, as local debts and interest translated into dollars on the parent company books will be greatly reduced. Also, as previously mentioned, you will likely be repaying the debt in currency worth far less than that you borrowed.

You will naturally have to deal with local banks; taking out financing just establishes you as an important customer. Be careful in less-developed areas, however, for you are treading where government and business overlap, and where people in power may also be in business.

In Chapter 5 we discussed hard currency versus soft currency in some detail. Any business will need hard currency to import needed materials and to repatriate dividends. Obtaining it in countries whose own currency is not accepted on the world stage can be difficult, and a good relationship with the leading local or central bank in such a country is essential.

DEVELOPMENT BANKS

Loosely associated with the United Nations are the World Bank and the International Monetary Fund, two large, powerful organizations whose purpose is to assist in development in the less-modern areas of the world. In addition, there are four regional development organizations with similar objectives. This is one of the unique sources of financing available to you.

The World Bank (or the World Bank group, as some refer to this giant), is the most widely known. The primary goal of the World Bank and its affiliates is to raise the standards of living in developing countries. The bank finances a broad range of capital infrastructure projects, but particularly focuses on investments that improve the quality of life of the masses. It also promotes economic development and structural reform in the countries in which it is involved. You may hear the term "structural reform" often. To me, it implies helping the developing country put into place the needed economic policies and organizations that will allow it to grow in the modern economic world. This entails support of the free-market system and of private enterprise. Occasionally, news articles report demonstrations or riots in countries where price controls have been lifted from commodities such as food. Such decontrol is often the result of the country's attempt to move toward a more open-market economy, in part to comply with requirements from the World Bank or other institutions such as the International Monetary Fund, which is discussed later in this section.

There are several units to the World Bank group, and if you are interested, you can pursue them at the contacts given in the Appendix. Two parts of the bank, the International Bank for Reconstruction and Development, founded in 1945, and the International Development Association (IDA), founded in 1960, lend funds, give advice, and try to get investments moving, with the IDA specifically concentrating on the poorer countries and providing easier financial terms. An affiliate, the International Finance Corporation (IFC), relates directly to the private sector. It invests its own funds as well as seeking out other monies for commercial enterprises. Another World Bank affiliate, the Multilateral Investment Guarantee Agency (MIGA), seeks to protect the investor from political risks. MIGA is discussed later.[1]

The World Bank is a huge operation, with more offices in Washington than can easily be counted. The bank names its buildings by letters of the alphabet, apparently in hopes of not forgetting any. This is a big bureaucracy, staffed with professionals from throughout the world, but it is indeed interested in helping the countries with which it works and has very real clout. The bank will talk to you, and may produce or lead you to your needed financing.

The other financial institution with worldwide scope is the International Monetary Fund, or IMF. This organization oversees the international monetary system and aids countries in their participation in that system in such areas as currency exchange-rate stability and balance-of-payments difficulties. My experience is that the IMF too is involved in advising governments on steps to improve their financial footing and economic success, as well as in structural reform.[2]

Clearly the World Bank and the IMF both have as general objectives economic growth and stability in the countries in which they are involved; they also work closely together. In countries throughout the world, you may meet with World Bank or IMF staff. They are often looking for help in arguing private-enterprise and/or market economy issues with skeptical government leaders, and they will likely look upon you as a potential ally in this effort.

In your dealings with both of these giant organizations, you will encounter a broad range of individuals. Some will readily identify with your interests whereas others will be academic, macroeconomic thinkers whose focus is on broad social issues rather than on concerns primarily of interest to specific businesses. I have seen members of these organizations be of great help in difficult international situations, such as when a despotic leader was putting local businesses under extraordinary pressures. I have also seen esoteric projects proposed by their staffs that could not stand up in the world of real business and government. Once, a project was put forward to bring all members of an industry together to focus on a particular continent and its need for that industry, the idea being that the member companies would pool their data and that bright analysts could then determine how best to service the continent, national borders aside. This project and its backers overlooked the fact that member companies of an industry are also intense competitors unlikely to share data, and that the many countries of the continent might look askance at an international organization ignoring their sovereignty and boundaries.

On a regional scale several development banks should be considered; contact details are given in the Appendix. These include the Asian Development Bank, the African Development Bank, The Inter-American Development Bank, and the European Bank for Reconstruction and Development. These are real development banks interested in real projects. Membership in the regional banks is held by modern industrial countries such as the U.S. and Western European nations, which largely provide the financing, and the so-called borrower members, the countries in the region needing the help.

The Inter-American Development Bank (IDB) was established in 1959 and focuses on economic and social development in Latin America and the Caribbean. The IDB supplements private funds as needed to support development in the borrowing member countries. The IDB too has its head offices in Washington, D.C., and also has offices throughout the borrowing member countries. As with the World Bank and the IMF, it may provide technical advice to the governments of the countries in which it is working. Projects are all over the lot, and include sewage treatment, road construction, support for entrepreneurs, education and training, farming, fishing, and so on.[3]

The European Bank for Reconstruction and Development (EBRD) is a recent entry into the field of major development banks. It was formally established in 1991 to aid in the development and transition of the countries of Central and Eastern Europe, and the former Soviet states, as they move to more market-oriented economies. The bank seeks to promote private initiative. It can make loans to private enterprise, invest in equity capital, make guarantees, and more.[4]

The African Development Bank, based in Abidjan in the Ivory Coast and with an office in Washington, seeks to aid the development of African member nations by financing projects and promoting private investment in Africa, among other things. Related to the bank is the African Development Fund, which provides financing to the poorer countries of Africa at especially low rates.[5]

The Asian Development Bank is much like the rest and is based in Manila, in the Philippines. With the great progress in several Asian countries, this bank should be able to sharpen its focus to specific needy nations in the area.[6]

In addition to being possible financing sources, directly or indirectly, the international development banks through their many projects also offer numerous supply opportunities for equipment manufacturers, engineers, consultants, construction firms, and similar businesses. The banks produce publications indicating their procurement needs, and these may be obtained through the contacts identified in the Appendix.

Aid Programs

There are numerous programs conducted by countries around the world to provide various forms of aid to needy lands. This aid might take the form of financial credits that the recipient country can use to buy needed equipment or material. In some lands this is the way branches of foreign operations keep going. The aid may also take the form of direct grants for purchasing commodities.

The U.S. Agency for International Development (US-AID) is the agency within the U.S. government that oversees most foreign aid of the United States. You might think that an American would have his or her best chance dealing with the USAID program, and this may someday become reality. The sad fact is that in the past, USAID has been staffed with people not necessarily interested in benefiting American companies. I recall a story about a major African country that was a USAID recipient. The manager of a subsidiary of a European company in the country called his counterpart at an American competitor, in effect to apologize for arranging for USAID to fund the import of a huge amount of its product into the cash-poor country. This was obviously a boon to the European company and a source of considerable irritation to the American. The USAID staff couldn't even understand the concern of the American company. It is of course wonderful to help people in needy lands, but by now the hope is that USAID is awakening to the possibility that helping those lands while using American companies is a more appropriate mission. There are signs that this may be happening.

Certainly, aid operations based in European countries and Japan seem less likely to make such an error. Countries that are the major competitors of the U.S. in international business have in the past at times tied their aid efforts to business ventures that in some manner benefited their own companies. This is a very real feature of international competition. Japan and many European nations seem to be involved in such support for their businesses abroad, and this form of aid, which requires the use of companies from the donor country, is popularly referred to as "tied" aid.

Another feature of aid programs is that some developed countries seem to "adopt" certain needy countries. In such instances, you may find yourself having to deal with the aid program of a major foreign government, as this is really the only significant aid source for the country in question. Dutch AID, for example, has focused on some African countries.

Within USAID, the Center for Trade and Investment Services is a good point of contact for business. Although recognizing the caution given earlier in this section, you nevertheless may be able to develop further financial leads through USAID and to supply some of the goods purchased by countries receiving USAID funding. The use of aid funds is not the way to finance a new operation, but it may keep your operation going if the host country encounters difficult financial straits.

THE U.S. GOVERNMENT

Several other areas within the U.S. Government might help with financing. In exporting goods and services from the U.S., a well-known supporter is the Export–Import Bank, also known as Eximbank, which since its founding in 1934 has helped finance more than $270 billion in U.S. sales abroad. This organization provides funding to help American goods compete in foreign markets, and does this by making it easier for foreign buyers to purchase American goods. Eximbank helps buyers of U.S. goods around the world obtain financing, and helps U.S. exporters with their export-related working-capital financing. It has recently undertaken a significant effort to aid small American businesses in their export efforts and has a toll free telephone number for this program. The bank has offices around the U.S. as well as in Washington.[7]

(Appropriate contacts for this organization and others cited throughout the chapter are given in the Appendix.)

The U.S. government publishes a directory of its resources to help U.S. businesses with exports. Entitled *Export Programs, a Business Directory of U.S. Government Resources,* it gives a lengthy list of contact points for export questions, and can be obtained through the Trade Information Center.

The U.S., in addition to its basic foreign-aid program, is also very active in specific countries, notably Israel and Egypt. If you have projects for these areas, you might even call on the appropriate State Department official to see what might be possible. The Commerce Department also has regional desk officers that support exporters.

The U.S. also offers insurance against unusual risk through the Overseas Private Investment Corporation (OPIC), which is discussed later.

You may have already noticed a strong focus on trade support in the U.S. government. Although this is highly valuable, I maintain that it is also an indication that the government lags considerably behind the realities of modern international business. Many American businesses may indeed wish solely to engage in selling wares abroad, but as indicated in Chapter 4, this is the lowest level of involvement in international business. To capitalize on the great growth markets of today and those that are just beginning to emerge will require far more than simply trying to sell U.S. goods to foreign customers. American companies must get involved in business in those foreign lands; in marketing, in manufacturing, and in serving the needs of local customers. That is, after all, exactly what they do in the U.S. The world is rapidly becoming a small global market to the international business community, even if the international governmental community lags decades behind.

As I have suggested, you will not get the same level of government support in your foreign efforts that competitors from Japan, Italy, France, and several other modern lands receive. Those countries' governments interpret the activities and successes of their companies abroad as an essential part of their foreign policy, as well as an important contribution to their own economic health, and they behave accordingly. I believe they are correct; their support often wins big contracts for companies from their countries, and American companies can do little about the situation. I recall another situation some time ago where a combine of American and British companies were outbid for a project in a developing country by an Italian company that bid almost twice the necessary project cost, but that also brought to the country extraordinary financing terms, such as no principle payments for years and almost no interest charge. American companies have no competitive recourse in such situations, although I hope Washington someday awakens to the need to support its companies more strongly. In the past few years there have been efforts in the State Department to train the heads of the embassy commercial sections in international trade, but much work remains. An embassy's formal purpose is diplomacy; nevertheless, with modern communications and instantaneous contact between an embassy and Washington, has not the promotion of American business become at least equal in importance to any other embassy purpose? Surely this must be so in all but the true hot spots. Diplomatic and commercial objectives are increasingly interconnected.

LOCAL GOVERNMENT

Depending on the size of your proposed business endeavor (and perhaps on unique factors associated with having that business in a foreign country), it may be possible for you to negotiate some really beneficial arrangements with the local government. This is discussed in Chapter 9 but noted here, as local governments themselves are a source of financing in the sense that you may be able to negotiate highly favorable entry terms, such as tax holidays. Especially in the less-developed and smaller countries, the local government may very much want you to enter and may be very willing to talk about possibilities. The formal governmental and corporate structure in such countries is not as rigid as that in the modern, developed world, and this flexibility often leads to an attractive venture.

PARTNERS AND OTHER PRIVATE SOURCES IN THE COUNTRY

Depending on the country, there may be private sources of significant funds. In Chapter 4 we looked at obtaining reliable partners in the country. These partners likely will be a potential source of funding, either by loaning the enterprise needed money or through acquiring equity. Beyond partners, there may be other private local sources. For modern countries, investment bankers in the U.S. may be able to give you contacts, or perhaps the local branches of major banks such as Citibank, Barclays, or Deutsche Bank can offer leads. In less modern lands, the local American Chamber of Commerce should be able to offer guidance to local sources of funds. So should the managers of foreign affiliates in the country if they do not think they will be in direct competition with you. No matter how poor the country, it seems it always has a few citizens with abundant resources. The U.S. embassy is also a potential source of such information.

As another possibility, you might consider financing by individuals throughout the world who invest in attractive projects, such as wealthy Middle Eastern businessmen.

OTHER SOURCES

Certainly don't forget to ask your primary bank; they may surprise you. The ambassador from the host country to the U.S. may have valuable insights, as may the U.S. ambassador in that country. The country desk officers in the U.S. State and Commerce Departments as well as the Office of the U.S. Trade Representative are potential sources of other leads, as are industry, finance, and trade departments in the government of the host country.

MIGA/OPIC

The World Bank and the U.S. government have taken steps to encourage investment in politically risky lands by establishing "insurance" programs. Specifically, these provide some financial protection against takeover (expropriation), against war and related political risks, and against the inability to convert local currency into hard currency for remitting profits. MIGA is the Multilateral Investment Guarantee Agency of the World Bank; OPIC is the Overseas Private Investment Corporation of the U.S. government. OPIC also provides loan guarantees and direct loans to U.S. investors undertaking international business activities. Contacts for both are given in the Appendix. These two organizations offer real protection to prospective operations in risky areas, and if you are interested in such places, you will want to speak to them.

CONCLUSION

Never be discouraged by wondering where the funds will be found. There are enough possibilities to keep you busy investigating for a long time indeed.

8

WHO ARE YOU COMPETING WITH?

If you have been in business for long, either as an individual or as a member of a larger company, you know about competition American style. You know there are always competitors trying to capture the sale that might be yours, offering lower prices or marginally different products, always hustling, using any business connections or advertising ploy they can find. They work long hours, just as you do, and everyone has one thing in common: You all understand the rules. Maybe you didn't when you first started, but you do now. Not only do you know the rules, you play hard within them. You know that you can't agree to buy a long-term supply of goods or services from one company in return for selling them your products. You know you can't agree with competitors to fix prices. You know you can't bribe a government official to get him to award a contract to your firm. You know what you can do. (Although a few business people unfortunately may at times choose not to follow all of the rules, they still surely know them.)

In foreign countries, you do not know all the rules. Some countries are so similar to the U.S. that you will think you do, but you won't. You will encounter competitors and competitive behavior that you most likely will never have seen before. Everyone will still be playing hardball, but by their own standards. In this chapter we will look at various types of competitors and their behavior.

KNOWING THE ROPES: THE ADVANTAGE OF THE LOCAL COMPANY

In Chapters 2 and 3 we looked at cultural differences and similarities between Americans and citizens of other countries, focusing on business in particular. From there we considered how to start business in a country, and aspects of working in soft currency, getting money out, and financing your efforts. By now you no doubt recognize that many problems you will face stem from ignorance of the local system and of getting things done. Companies staffed, managed, and owned by local citizens will have this advantage over you, and it is a significant edge, although not unassailable. Consider the Japanese and their success in the U.S.; certainly they did not understand our system when they started, but they do now.

Suppose you wish to obtain work permits for key employees to be brought into the country. You obtain forms from the appropriate agency and fill them out. Then everything stops. Government bureaucracy is slow everywhere. How do you get the agency to move? Without anyone on your side with the ability to understand and influence it, maybe you won't. You may wait months or years for approval. Your project may die while you wait.

There is a great need in such a case for a local expert, a fixer, someone who knows how the government works and who to talk to in the bowels of the bureaucracy to get things moving. He can decide if you have a chance. Such fixers do nothing illegal; they just know how to get things done. They also exist everywhere. In American companies they can get paper moved from department to department; in the U.S. government, they can get something to the right official's attention. You will need fixers. Earlier I recommended obtaining a local counsel; he may be the fixer for most things, and may have advice about others to hire. There are many needs for this expertise; indeed, you can't operate without it in most of the world.

As another example, suppose you need to import materials into a country. Will they make it into the country on time and in good shape? There had better be someone to check this out. You need a shipping expediter, a local who knows the ins and outs of the customs system, both the actual operations and the paperwork requirements. Expediters know the people and the system on the docks, how it really works; they may even be on hand when your material arrives. In many nations they had better be.

The National Company

In many areas of the world there is a national company in many industries . This is an organization owned by the state and reporting to a senior government official. The most obvious are those in the mining and energy areas, but for some countries this extends across the board, especially in the evolving countries of Eastern Europe and the former Soviet Union. In fact, in some countries of

Eastern Europe more than 90 percent of industry has been in government hands.[1] Since being freed from Soviet domination, these nations have been offering some state companies to private investors. Such sales will continue for years.

These national companies are to be found in poor lands, such as Zaire; in developing ones, such as Argentina; and in even more established countries such as France, Britain and, yes, the United States. Just because you haven't encountered one in your area of interest doesn't mean such creatures don't exist here; consider the U.S. Postal Service, for example.

Even in the most sophisticated environment, the national company is part of the government and reports to someone in it. In the energy industry, for example, the company may report to someone who regulates that industry for all participants. In an ideal country, this government official could not be influenced by the needs and performance of the national company. In less than ideal places, especially if the company reports at a high level, such influence is very apparent. The chairman of the national company may likely be a politician appointed by the current regime. He knows how the system works and to whom he is beholden, and he may have his eye on future positions. This situation exists throughout the world, in Africa in countries such as Zaire, Ghana, and Egypt; in the Middle East, for example in Saudi Arabia and Iraq; in Latin America in Mexico, Argentina, Venezuela, and Brazil; and in Russia and Eastern Europe.

The greatest problem will lie in the developing countries, where the government is controlled by a few and where a crafty minister has the ability to make or to sway decisions on price controls, contract awards, investments, and more.

Whether in a modern or a developing country, if your business happens to be in an industry that is in some way regulated by the national or state government, you will quickly see how a national company may have an edge. Such a company will get its opinions across to the regulator and those in authority more readily and easily than a foreign-owned company will. Despite the efforts of the World Bank and the IMF, prices and the supply of essential goods in many developing lands still are regulated by the government.

None of this means that you or your company cannot do well in such a situation. Government operations almost by definition are less efficient than private enterprises; indeed, my experience is that almost everywhere, private operations run competitive circles around the national company. Nevertheless, you must be aware of the influence held by the latter. In some instances, this works to the industry's advantage. Suppose a regulated industry feels justified in a price increase. Most likely the national company will have the lowest profit performance and therefore its books may be the best support for the industry's request. Prices are then raised by the regulatory authority to the benefit of all.

One other aspect of a government-owned corporation deserves note. In poorer lands, your national-company competitor may suddenly receive the direct or indirect benefit of attractive financial support or even equipment aid from a modern-country donor; after all, it is part of the government.

In recent years, especially with the breakdown of world communism and the growing respect for private enterprise, there has been a rush in many lands to privatize government holdings. In reality this is just in the beginning stages worldwide. The current privatization efforts, which likely will continue through the nineties, offer both vast opportunities and grave risks to American business. Privatization is explored in Chapter 9, which deals with unique opportunities.

INVOLVEMENT OF PROMINANT POLITICAL LEADERS WITH COMPETITORS

Foreign governments do not necessarily have the same perception of antitrust, price fixing, conflict of interest, and so on as does that of the U.S. Most European nations generally view such issues as we do, but not always, and other countries may have very different ideas. Even if a government official is expressly prohibited from being involved in business, he may find an indirect means to that end. This happens frequently in the third world. Your manager in a developing country may hear a rumor that one of his major competitors is in fact owned by a senior government official; or he or she may be even more surprised when that official or an aide provides that information directly.

In smaller countries leaders may exert unusual pressure on your operation. You may feel you do not have much control over key decisions, such as bringing in needed materials, setting prices, establishing policies for operation, or even hiring a senior local employee. This may be related to outside involvement on the part of the official, or he may indeed be pursuing some other political objective. Chapter 12 looks at this.

Related to general difficulties involving government officials is the judicial system. In most countries you should not rely on the local judicial system to resolve major disputes. In the modern lands of Western Europe this may be possible, but not in many other places. In more underdeveloped societies, attorneys and courts are not very prevalent. For the most part, however, the plain fact is that local interests will naturally have a clear edge over yours. Even if those in the judiciary are totally above-board, they cannot help being biased against an American operation in favor of local people and concerns. In many cases, even the appearance of impartiality may be hard to find.

Again, this is an area in which astute local advice is needed. Your local counsel and your senior local employees should have insights into the judiciary.

COMPETING AGAINST AFFILIATES OF FOREIGN COMPANIES IN THE HOST COUNTRY

One surprise for American business people is that they have to be alert to unorthodox behavior by prominent non-American international firms. The behavior of Americans and their companies is controlled by the Foreign Corrupt Practices Act. Aside from personal moral convictions, U.S. businesspeople are prohibited from offering bribes to a foreign official to influence decisions affecting business. This act and its influence on your behavior is covered in Chapter 11. As an illustration of behavior by a non-American company, I recall the rumor that a major firm, engaged in competitive bidding in a small land, offered its ruler a position with the company following the completion of his term in office.

American firms also will often find themselves competing against non-American firms on a legal but nonlevel playing field. As noted, many modern countries such as Italy and Japan aggressively back their companies in international business efforts, far more than the U.S. does with American companies. Such nations evidently believe the activities of their companies to be part of their foreign relations, their economic programs, and even their long-term security.

Such nations often provide incredibly low-cost financing for projects involving their companies, which encourages the host countries to award their business accordingly. The last chapter noted a case in which a European company was awarded a major project apparently because its bid brought with it the promise of almost-free financing from its home country. The European country saw the project as good for its economy, providing a boost for its company and jobs for its people at home and abroad. Obviously, government and business work together very closely in some lands.

As described in Chapter 11, groups of business leaders in Japan may meet frequently to discuss business issues of importance, a type of seeming collusion that just could not happen in the U.S. Although applicable laws are on the books even in Japan, there is clearly some question as to how strictly they are observed.

9

UNIQUE
OPPORTUNITIES

Aside from the questions of a country's growth rate, market potential, and the stability of its currency, another aspect of attractiveness should not be overlooked. A country may be especially attractive for your business even though it ranks poorly in terms of the other attributes discussed in this book. Perhaps there is such an abundance of a raw material your industry needs that you drool at the prospects of being involved, but the country is wretched, the laws are primitive, and you may never be able to get an operation started or staffed. This is a unique opportunity. The Middle East has represented a unique opportunity to the oil and gas industry for much of this century. The abundance is startling, but the environmental, political, social, and legal difficulties were (and continue to be) great.

There are many stories of companies that have been able to work their way through difficult situations that offer an extraordinary benefit. The original partners of

Aramco in Saudi Arabia certainly benefited greatly. Are there such opportunities out there for you or your company? Let's examine a few, and consider the inherent risks. For the most part, unique opportunities appear not to lie in the modern industrialized countries so much as in the developing ones. Although you may discover some in the modern lands, it is easier to see them in areas not so highly developed.

RAW MATERIAL ABUNDANCE

This is the most obvious unique opportunity. A country may be especially blessed in its supply of a raw materials. Copper in Zambia and Peru comes to mind, as do coal in the United States, diamonds in South Africa or Sierra Leone, and opals in Australia.

The oil example is obvious to most people. Certainly Saudi Arabia is not an easy land for Americans to work or live in, yet many American and other non-Saudi companies have operated there for decades. These include the major oil companies and a long list of others involved either in the oil industry—such as equipment suppliers—or in bringing the Saudi infrastructure up to modern standards, for example by providing a water supply, roads, schools, hospitals, and airports.

Currently the oil industry is investigating Russia and other recently opened lands of the former Soviet Union in an effort to capitalize on the great abundance of petroleum reserves in that area. This is a good example of what the risks are. You might have expected to see many announcements of companies signing multibillion-dollar deals with Russia, but the political instability there, the great distances from the oil fields to the ports, the enormous costs, and the general confusion of the country all lead companies to hesitate. There is indeed a great supply, but the potential costs and pain are very apparent, and as a result the pace of such project announcements has been slower than might have otherwise been expected.

In Ghana, abundant hydroelectric power and low labor costs led to the construction of a major aluminum plant, even though the plant is far from any sizable markets. The economics of the power source and the labor made this a unique opportunity.

In some instances, abundant raw material is located in a tightly controlled country, and it may not be easy to get involved. Certainly this is true of countries that nationalize what they perceive as key industries. As long as such control continues, there may not be much you can do; but the world is changing.

PEOPLE AVAILABILITY

This is a benefit of the less developed nations. Highly populous countries that are just embarking on the development road can often offer numerous people who will work for a fraction of the wages paid in modern countries. Of course, such workers also usually need training. China, Mexico, and other Latin American countries are examples of this, as is the Philippines. If you have an operation that is not high tech, these places provide significant benefits, and the countries will be happy to see you employ a large number of people. Of course, as noted for China in Chapter 1, such nations would prefer your industry to bring higher tech skills along with the jobs.

Training requirements are discussed in the next chapter, but suffice it to say that there are some very modern plants in terribly poor countries. Once a country begins moving steadily down the development road, the number of citizens trained by foreign industries increases steadily, and a skilled labor pool develops. Singapore is the greatest example, but Mexico provides similar cases. A German car manufacturer in Mexico actually ships some of its products home to Germany for sale because the quality and costs are so competitive. Developing countries today are very interested in the training that foreign companies can bring, and especially in the technology transfer to and employment of their citizens.

Privatization

Many of today's unique opportunities are coming from recent gigantic political changes. With the fall of communism and subsequent dissolution of the Soviet Union, not only the former Soviet states but also the countries of Eastern Europe have embarked on great change. This is also true for the many countries around the world formerly supported by the Soviets. They are all trying to become more economically viable, and this means (even though some may not be happy at the requirement), becoming more skilled at private enterprise. Many nations that had controlled much of their industry are now involved in selling state companies to private owners. They hope to improve their country's competitiveness by these sales, often acting with the guidance of the IMF, the World Bank, and numerous Western business consultants. The sales also bring in cash that is used to reduce the countries' debts.

Many countries in Latin America and Africa are also engaged in such privatization, not just those formerly associated with the Soviet Union. One very interesting case is Argentina. In an effort to copy the success of Chile and the recent improvements in Mexico, Argentina is trying to modernize as quickly as possible. Many firms already have been privatized.

These state sales are being made in places as diverse as Nigeria, Mexico, and Eastern Europe. Someone has to take advantage of these fire sales, and why not you? Be aware, however, that although there may be a few real buys here, there are also some incredible dogs, and you may be inheriting operations that have great inbred difficulties.

The companies being sold range from the very expensive to the small, so varied opportunities are available. You can obtain the latest list of such companies through each country's embassy in the U.S. The advice here is obvious: Investigate, investigate, investigate before buying.

Much has been written in the press in recent years about these privatization efforts; the telephone companies in Latin America are an example, including those in Chile, Mexico, Argentina, and perhaps now Brazil.[1] These are big steps, as was Mexico's privatization in 1991–92 of eighteen commercial banks, which brought the country $12.4 billion.[2] The recent selling of some shares of the national oil company YPF in Argentina, moreover, was to some observers precedent setting.[3] The great bulk of privatization worldwide still lies ahead, in the remaining years of the twentieth century. There are an enormous number of candidates available. As already noted, in Eastern Europe the majority of all industry has been held by the state.

Not all privatization opportunities are in developing lands. France has recently announced plans to privatize several of its prominent national firms, such as the drug company Rhone-Poulenc and the oil company Elf-Acquitaine.[4]

FINANCIAL SUPPORT AND SERVICES

A unique opportunity lies in the financial-support area. Depending on the industry and the country, the major development banks may be especially interested in your project. The World Bank, for instance, may have projects in mind for a particular developing country, and if your industry happens to fit with one of those, you may have a ready source of financing. You will never know unless you check with the bank, so I suggest looking into what this bank and similar institutions are doing in the countries of your interest, especially if you are involved in the developing countries.

In a different area (and as an opportunity), the financial-services field is crying for help in many developing countries. Consider the nations of Eastern Europe, and the former Soviet Union members: They do not have the background to easily become globally competitive in financial services. Banking services, equity financing, and stock markets are all fascinating, new, and puzzling, and such areas must develop for the countries to modernize. Some international institutions such as Citibank and Deustche Bank are actively getting involved, but this will certainly be an attractive area for years to come. Even the concept of a commercial bank loan is difficult to grasp and pursue if there has never been such a thing.

MARKET OPPORTUNITIES

In almost all cases, you will naturally be looking at market attractiveness, so why is this listed as a unique opportunity? The answer is that there are a few countries whose size alone makes them unique opportunities for some industries. China and India are two, being the most heavily populated countries on earth; as noted, together they hold 40 percent of the people on the planet. Each is overcoming a history of backwardness, and is growing far more rapidly than the modern West recognizes. Indeed, since 1980, China and India have been among the fastest-growing economies on earth. These countries still are fraught with problems, social strife, and political systems and institutions trying to come to grips with the modern world. They have years of serious problems ahead. Nevertheless, this is where the people are.

Are you interested in making or selling products that might be bought by people in these countries? Mass-market products that appeal to these citizens and that are relatively inexpensive might score a big success. Of course, you may have some difficulty getting into business in these countries, as they are more interested in technology transfer, in upgrading the skills of their people, and in providing jobs. If you can provide jobs for a significant number of people and bring training as part of the business you have a real chance.

As another possibility, even if you are not in the mass-market business, the sheer size of these countries and their growing economic clout means that they can buy staggering amounts of big products and high-tech equipment, even though on a per-citizen basis such expenditures may not seem that large. Airplane sales to China are an example.

Each year the U.S. government goes through a hand-wringing exercise over whether to continue China's most-favored-nation status, which is given to most of our trading partners; human rights continue to be the sore point. Those desiring to expand business relationships argue that Americans can influence a country more by being involved there than by staying outside. Nevertheless, you as a businessperson need to realize that this is a political risk area. Will the actions of the U.S. government suddenly harm your business activities? American companies have always faced this risk abroad, because the U.S. more than European countries uses the economic stick to gain political objectives. Chapters 11 and 12 explore this issue. It is unfortunate that the federal government is not as aggressive in using its political and economic clout to back the efforts of its companies.

Eastern Europe fits the unique market-opportunity group. Again, depending upon your business interests, countries such as Poland, the Czech Republic, and Hungary may offer great opportunities. You just need staying power, perseverance, and products they do not have and can't easily get. Knowledge and skill in Western capitalism are in this category, for example the financial services noted earlier.

We don't yet know what challenges the former Soviet Union members represent. They should be full of unique opportunities, and if you are an optimist, they are. You'll need stamina, as well as long-term hopes and objectives if these new countries are your target.

TOURISM

There are numerous spectacular places in the world that Westerners with money would love to visit, if they knew where to go and how to travel there safely. Many such places are in Africa. Zimbabwe has a burgeoning tourist industry, with wonderful places to stay amid water buffalo, elephants, and antelope in the wild. There are lakes in which I am sure the fish have never seen fishhooks; that certainly was my experience. If you are in this industry you should be creating relationships in such places, establishing spots that only you can offer travelers.

There are no more spectacular beaches than the wide, white ones of Sierra Leone, and other than a few French citizens, almost no one in the modern industrialized world knows they are there. The water is crystal clear, and you can walk seemingly forever. I recall ambling along into a tiny village on the shore, where the men had their hollowed log dugouts ready to go out into the ocean as needed. In Saudi Arabia friends and I once stumbled into an old village built of sand on a high bluff, an impressive city from which the country had been ruled in the past, and we realized that we were the only people there.

There are many such opportunities. The travel industry is missing a bet. Zimbabwe, Zaire, Zambia, Sierra Leone, Chile, Saudi Arabia, the Sudan; the list goes on and on. I recall being taken down to the Nile in Khartoum. We were going out in a small houseboat—the only boat on the Nile that day—and we walked through a rusty iron hulk that seemed to be a gunboat. Upon investigating we learned from the Sudanese that this was the gunboat that late in the last century Lord Kitchener had carried in pieces across the desert, reassembled, and taken up and down the Nile, firing at rebels in an effort to restore British control (the locals had some years earlier overthrown the British). This boat could have been in a museum, but it was just rusting on a riverbank in the Sudan. Of course, I could understand why the Sudanese might not want it in a museum.

NEGOTIATING THE UNIQUE OPPORTUNITY: SOME CAUTIONS

Looking for unique opportunities is intriguing. You will not be in the international business world for long before seeing some firm that has found such a beneficial niche. Even the most intransigent regime will listen to a proposition if there are sufficient benefits for it or for the country, so you can usually dream up a way to try to make a unique opportunity work. There are always carrots you can offer, such as training a large number of local citizens, beginning a business that will bring in hard currency by export sales, or providing some needed facility for the country. You should be careful with all this, however, and not be led away from your basic objectives.

It's important to guard against being overly impressed by first observations; Brazil is a case in point. You will very likely be impressed by the industrial might of this country. Driving from Sao Paulo to Santos, I was deeply impressed by the industrial infrastructure; indeed, it reminded me of some industrial areas of the U.S. Visitors to Brazil are also impressed by the beauty of Rio, the charming beaches, the attractive people, the pleasant cafes, the music, the size of the country, and much more.

But the Brazilian economy is complex, risky, difficult, and unstable. Time and again people have been misled. If you have nimble financial experts who can dance in financial terminology, and if you or other managers at home can tolerate high levels of risk and remain calm in the face of the strange things that happen on financial reports when inflation and devaluation are running wild, Brazil may be a place for you. If you are willing to put up with such strain and problems for a period of years in the hope that this country too may someday take the high road and join Chile, Mexico, and Argentina in their efforts to advance, there are indeed opportunities. It is not a place for the faint-hearted or for people who revel in stability and risk-free environments.

As another caution—and this point will be made throughout the book—no opportunity is worth the headaches, time, anguish, and risk that may come from working with unscrupulous people. If you encounter such people in power in any country, you should stay away. Certainly, difficult people and cultures may present great challenges; but if there is integrity among all involved, deals can be worked out. I am warning here of more than barriers erected by culture and tradition; I am warning about unscrupulous people that you cannot trust. You will not be able to structure documents to protect your operation or your staff sufficiently in such places. These people probably control the rules and the law.

CONCLUSION

There are so many opportunities out there it is difficult not to write forever. This chapter has pointed out a few unique ones, together with some cautions. Always keep your attention focused on your company's objectives. One great risk is to be led into a diversion, an attractive opportunity that because of its unique features ends up draining away the time and talent of both you and your company. Some problems that arise in difficult environments cannot, it seems, be permanently solved; they keep returning.

10

STAFFING YOUR FOREIGN OPERATION

When you have made your decision and are ready to begin business operations in another country, you may need people for sales, marketing, accounting, plant operating, maintenance, secretarial support, and so on. In any particular case you may need only a few of these skills, but this chapter will cover those necessary for a complete business operation.

Nothing is more crucial to the success of the new operation than the people that staff it. Depending on the sophistication and uniqueness of the business, employees may need a variety of particular skills.

It may surprise you to learn, then, that you may not have the freedom to staff your new operation as you wish. What do you do if the host country requires you to use only local labor and no one has the requisite skills? Alternatively, if you receive permission to bring in a talented staffer from outside the country, how do you entice that person to move to the new location, especially if it is a

rather primitive place without much cultural life outside of work? How do you take care of this employee's
family?

These are significant concerns that occur throughout
the world. Let's look at solutions.

LOCAL PEOPLE

Certainly if your operation is to be located in a modern
industrialized country—a Western European community,
Canada, Australia, Japan, or New Zealand—there will
probably be local people with the talents required. You
might have concerns about local work customs or worker
expectations, but at least this fundamental requirement
can be met. Somewhere in these countries are people who
know how to weld, who can balance the books, who can
write, and who can operate computers. In these countries
your concern is hiring local staff, and your focus is more
on working with local agencies and your own employees to
develop appropriate benefit packages and recruit the
needed people. Still, it should be noted that even in sophisticated Western countries, governments very much
wish to employ local citizens, and you will receive real "en-
couragement" along these lines. If the skills are available,
the economics of the situation will also strongly promote
the use of locals.

What about all the other countries of the world? You
surely noticed that the list of countries having a broad
range of talent available numbered only about twenty.
There are about two hundred countries in the world, now
that the Soviet Union has dissolved, and there are serious
staffing concerns in all the others.

First and foremost, if the modern nations wish foreign
companies operating in their borders to employ their

local citizens, the less-sophisticated countries feel even more strongly about this. In fact, countries having the least-developed labor pool probably feel the strongest and will therefore give you the greatest problems. Official labor policies dealing with the use of locals may be firmly established in formal regulations, but more likely will be enforced as basic business policy by the country's government through its industry, labor, or commerce department.

By now you may be frowning as you consider the problems you face, given your company's probable need for special talents. It is essential to face the fact that regardless of what you are going to be doing—from making soap to making computer chips, from selling cars to selling movies—you are going to be doing it with local citizens as your employees. There is a chance you can bring in one or two senior experts from your home office (and we will discuss this later), but most of your employees will be locals.

Immediately, another term pops into consideration: *training.* You may have been involved in training employees before, but you haven't seen anything yet.

Before getting too depressed over the requirement to hire locals and train, train, train, let's recognize that regardless of whatever business you are in, several areas of your operation should be staffed by locals even if you can bring in all outsiders. From the standpoint of effectiveness, your operation probably cannot be staffed without locals in the employee-relations area. It is also difficult to deal in the marketplace without those who understand local customs, needs, and business etiquette; so marketing people and most managers had better be locals. Furthermore, your affiliate will certainly need a senior manager with a serious title and a meaningful position who understands how the host government operates and how to get things done. In areas such as legal work, public relations, and supply, you cannot do without locals. Speaking economically, for that matter you cannot afford to staff your plant, warehouse, terminal, distribution center, or the like with anyone other than locals, or you will be economically uncompetitive from the beginning.

NEED FOR OUTSIDE EXPERTISE

Always remember, it is your operation, it is your money, and your company is taking the risk. Certainly in less-sophisticated countries you should position people who have the experience, knowledge, and integrity to handle the business thousands of miles away from the home base. The top manager—who may be called president, manager, general manager or whatever—as well as the top financial, marketing, and manufacturing managers should be appointed from your pool of company talent. If you fail to gain permission for all four, certainly you should strive for at least two of these. Any executive from outside a country at times needs a confidant off of whom to bounce ideas, especially in the more difficult nations of the world.

There are variations on these four positions. Because successful marketing depends so much on local market knowledge, you might choose to have a local in the top marketing position and bring in a skilled marketing person from the home office to work under him. I would never give up the top financial position, and would certainly strive to have the top executive position filled from outside. If you are engaged in manufacturing a sophisticated product, it is probably a bit easier to convince the local authorities to allow a work visa to your manufacturing executive.

If you are in fact constructing a massively expensive manufacturing facility requiring sophisticated technical knowledge and experience on the part of various plant foremen, operators, maintenance workers, and others, you may be successful in obtaining permission for bringing in more experts from outside the country to fill these spots, especially at start-up, but even in this there will likely be a time limit established by the government at which point these workers are to be replaced by locals. Even in a case like this, you may encounter the requirement that the majority of staff at start-up be locals. Training is a big, big word in foreign operations. One well-tried practice of companies put in this position is to overstaff such that many of the locals needing training are duplicated by experienced outsiders during the early months of operation. This works but will obviously influence the start-up economics.

The basic staffing strategy is to negotiate at the outset the positions that will be filled by outsiders. Naturally, this is much more important in countries having less-sophisticated labor pools, and in industries with more-sophisticated technical requirements. The local department of labor is generally involved in these issues, and sometimes the immigration or the commerce and trade departments. Each country has some department and senior official responsible for granting work visas to foreigners. You will be working with this person and department, probably through a local counsel or other expediter that you should employ early on. Again, there is no substitute for having an early relationship with a local adviser who knows how the country works, whom to contact, and how to get things done. The local embassy of the U.S. can advise on this, as can the local American Chamber of Commerce chapter, and executives of other foreign affiliates who, especially in difficult climates, seem to be willing to discuss this type of issue.

Above all, don't give up control of your operation; if that is the requirement, find another country.

TRAINING

This is an enormous subject and deserves its own book, but it can be broken into a few key considerations.

Training Needs for Operation in a Modern Industrialized Country

In this case the training needs are not greatly different than those you might experience opening an operation at a new site in the U.S. Required are familiarization with the unique aspects of the company, as well as any special needs of the manufacturing, marketing, and accounting operations; this can all probably be handled by existing training programs, by utilizing your own professionals and operators as trainers either at the new site or at home office (to which you may bring some of the new hires), or by putting some of the new employees in your existing operation in advance, so they can gain the needed knowledge.

All this is costly and takes effort, but it pales in comparison to the training requirements for new operations in the rest of the world.

Training Needs for Operation in Less-Developed Countries

Now we are referring not just to countries in Africa or the Middle East, but also to the rapidly growing counties of Asia/Pac Rim and in parts of Latin America. Most certainly we are referring to any operation being considered for Eastern Europe, and especially in the former Soviet states.

The great advantage held by some of the rapidly growing countries of Asia/Pac Rim is that many of their citizens have been trained by international firms already present. Second, some of these nations put great emphasis on education and training, and there may be a pool of talent available. Most probably, though, that pool is employed in good jobs already. Singapore is an example of this. The citizens are bright, extremely hard-working and industrious, and employed. You will have to steal some away from other companies or develop your own.

Training Requirements for Complex Operations   By this is meant operations involving the construction and start-up of complex manufacturing facilities, and also the marketing of highly technical products. It is impossible to train people in a week or two to occupy significant positions in such an operation; you must plan the employee-training program with care, thoroughness, and an eye always on its cost. Training costs can get out of hand quickly.

Certainly everyone wants to hire the best available people. Let's assume at the outset that you have done that. Let's further assume that (as indeed would be the case almost anywhere), the local country presses you to use an overwhelming majority of locals in your operation. Somehow you have to bring these people up to the necessary skill level.

Depending on the size of your operation and its projected attractiveness, there are alternatives. Surely the best is to bring newly hired employees occupying skilled positions to one of your existing operations, probably in the U.S., and train them with your staff. Best by far are programs in which the new people actually fill positions in those operations, perhaps with one of your veterans looking over their shoulders as you deem necessary.

The fact is that if you are in a sophisticated industry requiring operating knowledge in fields such as electronics, chemicals, or metallurgy, this training is going to require many months. If you are starting with educated employees who just don't have your specific industry knowledge, perhaps you can train supervisors and operators in six months. If you are starting with employees that have minimal relevant education, the time period increases greatly.

For professionals, if you are fortunate enough to hire qualified locals, the approach should be much the same. Ideally, you should bring the professionals to work with one of your existing operations for some time.

The cost of all this is considerable, of course. Another approach is to staff your operation in its early days with as many of your own veterans as possible, putting the local hires into some kind of work relationship with them whereby they can learn on the job without destroying the operation. This may require setting up local formal training courses, or utilizing local facilities in countries that have them; most of all it will necessitate your negotiating at the outset with local authorities for permission to bring in your veterans for the necessary time.

Less-Complex Operation Requirements and On-Site Training If the operation being established does not deal in highly technical products or require sophisticated manufacturing knowledge, the training problems are much smaller. The most economic approach is to train on site utilizing local talent plus outside experts flown in for particular subjects, as well as any outsiders you already have in the country. You can take a few key new employees offshore to one of your operations for hands-on training. The people would be those with the highest potential, the ones you expect to fill supervisory roles and be capable of passing on their training to others.

On-site training is also necessary in more complex operations, as no company can afford extended offshore training. In countries without the approach of modern

Western society toward industry, skilled veterans of your company should serve as on-site trainers for the new employees. A marketing veteran could actually work with local people in sales efforts. Learning by doing on site is a time-honored, effective way of training that far surpasses classroom approaches for certain cultures.

Classroom training generally is of value only in imparting needed academic skills in seriously deficient areas.

Cultural Leap   In many countries, bringing local people into your operation, even if it is no more than a local sales office, brings them into firsthand participation in a world they have never known.

This is not the case in the modern countries of the West, nor is it likely to be in the several booming economies of Asia/Pac Rim that soon will join the modern nations, but it is surely the case for the rest. For the really ancient societies into which the modern world is just now beginning to intrude, the leap is across centuries. This describes the Middle East, Africa, parts of Asia and Latin America, and many countries of the old Soviet Union and Eastern Europe. Training for these countries takes on a significance beyond the comprehension of normal business. I recall an engineer associate from a Middle Eastern country who was working on a project in the United States. When he went home, he flew from this modern world across the ocean into his country, at which point he changed clothes, rented a four-wheel drive, and headed out into the desert to find his mother, who lived in a tribe of bedouins that moved about the land. He didn't cross just a few thousand miles when he flew home: He crossed ages.

Chapter 2 deals with such cultural issues, but if you really contemplate a significant operation in a nation such as this, think seriously about the differences and the burdens they will bring to your company and your employees. You should discuss such issues not only with embassy staffs but also with academic experts on the country in question, and most importantly, with executives of other foreign operations in that country, if there are any.

BRINGING IN OUTSIDE EXPERTISE

Enticing one of your trusted and talented employees to uproot his or her life and move to a foreign land is difficult under almost any circumstance. It is much easier if the destination is Britain or France, or for some individuals even Japan. It is extraordinarily difficult if the destination is Zaire, Zambia, Colombia, or Myanmar (Burma). For the few attractive spots to which some people will actually jump to relocate, considerations revolve around the employee's family and the economics of the move. For the other countries, enticement becomes a real concern, especially living conditions and rewards.

Family Concerns

In the U.S. today more and more professionals are in marriages in which both partners work in serious careers. When one partner is offered an attractive promotion at a good salary even in an exciting and interesting spot in the world, it is increasingly difficult for that person to accept the offer if this means a long-term separation from the family, or if the spouse must give up his or her career. I know of instances in which the employee does go in single status, but considering the extended time commitment and the social demands on a top manager in many foreign lands, this is not really a satisfactory answer.

Critical to the employee's agreeing to such a move is the quality of the new location. Modern Western societies should not be so difficult to sell to employees, nor locations in the booming countries of Asia that are growing so rapidly. The family concerns for such spots revolve around whether quality education is available for the children, whether the spouse will be allowed to work (most probably not by local law), whether the financial support will allow the family to live in the quality to which they are accustomed, or at least comfortably and safely, and so forth. There are usually American or international schools in major cities but not in isolated areas, and there are usually other foreign residents in the large cities as well, so that for many spots there will be other citizens from the home country for support. If your operation is large and will have several employees from home, that in itself is a comfort.

If the move is to a less-sophisticated country, the married employee will have many family concerns:

- Are there appropriate schools? Sending children to boarding schools in countries far away from the family is not a step most Americans take eagerly.

- What are the health concerns? This is important in much of the world and is covered in some depth in Chapter 13.

- What about basic security? This too is fundamental, and is also covered in Chapter 13.

- Is there any social life? In many countries, the social life consists of entertaining in the home and visiting the homes of other foreign residents.

Job Concerns

Employees may look upon an assignment to a foreign locale as another positive punch to their career ticket up the line, or they may look at it as being dangerously out of the action, far removed from the group that is running the company. They may fear being forgotten. Their response in this area depends entirely on your company's attitude. If your international operations are small in comparison to the rest of the company, this fear may be very strong, unless it can be truthfully made clear that their accepting the offer and performing well in the foreign assignment will cause them to be seriously considered for subsequent promotional opportunities.

Economic Concerns to the Employee and to the Company

In the end, you are going to have to pay dearly to move employees and their families overseas. For the glamour spots such as Paris and London, there may not need to be much of a salary inducement, but just the cost to support a family in attractive conditions will be dear. London, Paris, and similar destinations are much more expensive than the U.S. As for other countries, the amount paid to attract employees and their families varies directly with the difficulty of the country. It will cost a bundle to move someone to Zaire.

What are you going to pay? Aside from basic salary, you will face providing a housing allowance that will likely be steep to provide anything close to the comfort of home. Also, there will be travel back home, at least once a year for a vacation and perhaps another time for a rest leave. If the assignment is to a particularly troublesome or dangerous area, you might have to give rest trips more frequently, for in such spots the employee is unlikely to have his family with him.

Since there is such a wide range of attractiveness of spots throughout, if your company becomes involved in sending people to more than one location, you will find it necessary to rank the areas in terms of livability, and pay premiums accordingly. It is, for example, more difficult for some spouses to live in Saudi Arabia than in London. A place like London might get a minimal such premium while a Middle Eastern location would get a higher one; more difficult African areas such as Khartoum or Kinshasa would require the greatest of all. A little realism will usually help you come up with a fair approach. One method is to imagine yourself and your family living in the country in question when your children are, say, eight and fifteen years old. How hard would that be? If you are honest with yourself, you will quickly be able to determine the true hardship posts.

One word of advice is called for. It never pays to save a few bucks in supporting families offshore. Unhappy employees, spouses, and children are a disaster. Remember, they are running your operation and representing your company and country in this foreign land.

Finding the Right Employee to Go

The best manager in your company, the hardest driver of his employees, the hardest worker—all these may be grand at home and disasters in some foreign assignments. Whoever is doing the selecting must become as familiar as possible with the requirements that will be placed on the employee and his family. In modern countries this might not be much different than at home, although in most places there will nevertheless be a new language and guaranteed cultural differences. Americans like the British because in part Americans think they both speak the same language. Even in Britain, it's tough at times. The British are not so immediately friendly as many Americans are, and the food is surprisingly different. Anyone going to live outside the U.S. is in for some strain, even in a wonderful place like Britain.

As for other lands, the employee and his family may encounter myriad problems that did not exist at home.

In the least-developed countries, hours are spent doing simple things, like ensuring an adequate supply of drinking water at home, obtaining a driver's license, or having a workman install a telephone (if this is even feasible). There may be minimal entertainment of the type Americans are used to. Television is poor; security may make trips out to movies a bit risky even if there are any; there may be only one or two good restaurants; there may be numerous frightening diseases such as malaria, river blindness, or bilharzia; and finally, Americans are indeed prey for terrorists in certain areas of the world.

The family may not even be able to keep teenagers at home, but may be forced to put them in boarding schools in Europe or the U.S. This may be due to local pressure (such as in Saudi Arabia, which does not like having American teenagers around), or perhaps to the parents' assessment that there are no quality schools in the country for the teenagers to attend. I have seen parents driven to distraction over troubled teenagers in distant boarding schools, trying to cope with them through headmasters, friends, or expensive trips.

Balancing all this are the wonders of life in different lands: new cultures, people, stories, foods, and adventures relatives and friends back home cannot imagine. How about going on a real safari, seeing an elephant graveyard, visiting Victoria Falls or the Great Wall of China, or the pyramids, or the ruins of Capernaum? How about dealing with the political and business leaders that run the countries? It's certainly possible in the smaller ones. These are inducements for some people and mean nothing to others.

Beyond all this there are cultural considerations. How will your employee fare in the culture of his assigned country? (Again, this subject is dealt with in chapter 2.) For example, it is hard to learn how to manage in a company in which employees will never object to a remark by the boss but always answer "yes" or nod even if they do not agree. It takes great sensitivity to communicate effectively in such a place. As another illustration, how is your top manager in the foreign land going to respond to extraordinary pressures from local governments, pressures that may be personally dangerous in some countries? Chapters 12 and 13 deal with this issue.

Consider employees to be assigned overseas carefully. It's all too easy to create the proverbial bull in a china shop.

The Home Office

Easily overlooked but very important is the quality of the managers and staff that your company will have back at the home office supporting and coordinating the international operations. Managers in foreign lands may develop a sense that the folks back at headquarters just do not know what is going on "out here," and to some extent they will be correct. The home-office executive responsible for the international operation absolutely must visit regularly to build up his own base of understanding, to visibly support the local managers and staff, and to establish credibility for his recommendations and guidance with both the foreign operation managers and the senior executives at home.

Similarly, home-support staffers that deal regularly with the foreign operation must develop their own understanding of the problems. This would include accountants, treasurers, employee-relations people, marketing and manufacturing advisers, and more. To the extent feasible and economical, people from these functions should visit the foreign operation. Efforts should be made to give a positive tone to this relationship in the early days, when people from the home office are likely on site involved in training new local employees and in other aspects of start-up. One warning: Home office managers and staff must always guard against coming across as all knowing. True, they may know more about the specific products, systems, and culture of the company, but the local staff surely knows more about the local situation, both its challenges and its opportunities. The headquarters support team must not make burdensome demands on the foreign operation, such as endless requests for information that is nice to know at headquarters but doesn't really mean a lot. In a foreign operation such requests may take an inordinate amount of time, as the local staff is probably not as large or sophisticated, and certainly not as knowledgeable in company culture and requirements. Besides, you want the talent in the foreign operation to be working on the real problems, getting the operation to run smoothly, making sales, and solving the horrendous local issues that the staff at home cannot easily comprehend.

In many smaller developing countries the manager of your local operation may find himself meeting frequently with government officials to discuss their concerns. He may also have to meet with officials who make unrealistic demands, especially if the government is involved through influential stockholders or the like. Local managers just do not have the same problems as the home-office staff.

One last point: Those working in the home office have the clear duty to keep senior management informed and educated to the extent necessary, but at the same time to shield foreign operations from needless incursions by senior executives. If the support staff has difficulty understanding the problems of the foreign operation, you can be sure the senior executives of the company who are involved only a few minutes a month have no real comprehension of the situation. Ideally, of course, some of them will have had experience in such operations, and this will help. Zaire, Colombia, France, and Singapore are not the United States.

CONCLUSION

It all comes down to people, their concerns and interests. Training, sensitivity, security, motivation, and understanding are people concerns. Always important in business in the U.S., they are magnified enormously in long distance, offshore operations.

People were always the key to any business and they still are.

11

THE ROLE OF GOVERNMENT

How do you regard Uncle Sam? Strictly from the perspective of the business world, how do you see the federal government? As a friend? As a supporter of your efforts to be successful? As an entity sincerely interested in doing what it can for your business to prosper?

If you were to go to meetings with government staff in Washington, do you believe they would understand your concerns?

Now, stop the snickering, and the impolite comments; I know. It's more like a bureaucratic dragon, eating away at your time and your attempts to succeed, increasing costs and draining profits that might be used to grow the enterprise. It's staffed by people who do not know what the business world is about and seem not to care. There are nice people that work there, to be sure, but the laws, regulations, and procedures were not designed with you in mind.

That's how you see the federal government as it relates to your business efforts in this country, isn't it? Requirements that do not increase productivity but just increase costs. Reports to be submitted endlessly on areas perhaps of interest to society but not to the guts of the business.

In most lands business people have some of those comments about their government. However (and this is a big however), for many of your potential international competitors from other modern nations, the government is a big supporter of their business community and works for its success; in less-developed lands, the government may actively participate in most major business decisions, whether good or bad.

Foreign governments are much more involved, and you will interact much more with those governments than you can imagine. In this chapter we will review the types of that involvement, and in the following chapter look into its risks.

PLANNED ECONOMIES

Some of the great economies of our day are planned, although not in the sense that the old Communist regime attempted to plan the Soviet Union's economy, controlling all details of production (and failing miserably). These leading economies are planned in a "consensus" manner, in working out agreements between the government and the business community on broad but very real common objectives. In the U.S. the concept of a planned economy is an anathema to both business and government, but not in Japan, the giant rival of the U.S. for world economic leadership. Nor is it in Singapore, the shining example of what creativity and hard work can do in the modern world. In both countries the national government sees the vitality and security of the country, the quality of life, indeed the success of the nation as tightly linked to the success of its business institutions. The governments work with the business world, whether to the delight or the consternation of business leaders. The two worlds do not always see eye to eye in these countries, but they do apparently recognize the same long-term goal.

In these lands, there is discussion between government and business leaders, there is respect for opinions, and there is adherence to goals. There is also understanding and compromise when conflicting objectives arise. Singapore is interested in many things, such as gaining increasingly high-tech industries, keeping its air and water quality high (and even improving it), educating its citizens, and much more. Nevertheless, it is not likely to pursue a secondary objective to the point of negatively affecting its vibrant and growing economy; all the country's advantages come from that. The government is set up and staffed by people who will make this overall goal happen. If you try to get into business in that country and are attractive to the government, you will be shocked at the support you receive.

In Japan, of course, you will face a much larger system, one in which there is already enormous strength in most areas. You will notice the great cooperation between business and government fostered, supported, and coordinated by MITI, the Ministry for International Trade and Industry, which is deeply involved in aiming the Japanese business machine in the right direction. You may also notice extraordinary cooperation among groups of companies. In Japan there are several major business groups known as *keiretsus*. These are loose conglomerations of companies across many industries, held together in part by common ownership of each other's stock. Periodically chief executives of the member companies of a keiretsu meet to discuss areas of interest, and lesser-level executives do likewise. Although adherents of U.S. antitrust policy would recoil in horror at this behavior, and though it is impossible to imagine such activity taking place in the U.S.,this is indeed a matter of course in Japan. Not all Japanese companies are members of keiretsus, but many are. Keiretsus seem to be fashioned either around major banks or around a large company and its suppliers. The Japanese MITI and keiretsus seem to have found a way to focus business and government in an efficient manner to emphasize strengths, get the most out of research, and capitalize on investment. It's a system that just does not fit under U.S. laws and practices.[1]

There are other models of course, in light of the success of these countries. Some countries try the Singapore model to some extent; indeed, I have always thought of Chile in some ways as the Singapore of South America. China surely is the largest planned economy today, and its steady economic growth since 1980 is evidence that something is working.

EUROPEAN COMMUNITY

Most countries in Europe are more like the U.S. than like Japan, but here too there is more government/business interaction than in the U.S. The monstrous efforts of the European Community bureaucracy to unify policies and bring member countries together into a viable economic union could not have proceeded so fast in recent years were this not so. Companies and whole industries meet with relevant E.C. directorates, such as those on environment or industry, to iron out policies and laws in ways that would not be tolerated by American business.

As already noted, the governments of individual European countries also go to great lengths to back efforts of their companies in foreign markets, providing project loans at terms that do not exist for competing American companies abroad. They—as does Japan—provide aid to developing countries that at times and in some manner seems to be tied to use of the country's companies.

LOCAL GOVERNMENT APPROVAL AND OVERSIGHT OF FOREIGN OPERATIONS

The influence and even control that the host government exerts over your prospective business operations in its country will nowhere be more evident than in your efforts to get your enterprise underway. Some of this involvement is expected; after all, even in the U.S. you have to obtain various approvals and licenses, and you may already have had experience dealing with the EPA, affirmative action, and the like.

But the extent of government control and influence in many foreign countries, especially the developing ones, may surprise you. As we saw in the last chapter, you may have difficulties staffing your operation as you would like. Many countries will absolutely prohibit your bringing in outside staff, hence forcing you to work with locals. To the extent that you must have outside expertise, approval will require skillful negotiations, and you may have to agree to other onerous requirements such as sending these staffers home as soon as you have trained locals.

Consider the financial area. First and foremost you will need currency acceptable on the world stage so that you can bring in needed materials. In any country without hard currency (and that means most of the world's countries), you will have to negotiate with the central bank for the amounts you need.

In your start-up negotiations, you may discover an interest on the part of the government in having a government-owned company as your partner. Another variation on this theme is partial ownership of the equity of your local operation by such a company.

Continuing this long list, what about price controls? In many nations the selling price of your goods may not be your decision. Guess who makes the decision?

What about the highly desired ability to repatriate profits to the U.S.? As Chapter 6 noted, this is not so easy in many countries, and again the government is the one in control.

In many countries the government has a clear plan for where it wants the country to go. This is, again, the case in Japan and Singapore, as it is to some extent in other lands such as Mexico, Chile, and Argentina. In such lands your business may have to be seen as fitting into the government plan. If your business is small, this is probably not a relevant issue, but if it is large, it may either be very much helped or harmed by the government's thoughts as to desirable business enterprises.

Beyond these specific areas, there is one of greater concern, which is discussed more in the next chapter. This has to do with the fact that in most developing countries there will be only a few officials who stand between you and getting your business started, and who have some ongoing role of monitoring or approval. They may exert unusual pressure on you, and you will have to decide how to respond. This pressure may vary from urging you to employ at a high level some out-of-work politician or relative, all the way to obviously corrupt requests. I would hope you are well grounded in your basic moral beliefs and understand applicable U.S. law before you get involved in any foreign business negotiations.

MEETING WITH DIGNITARIES

Throughout this book we have alluded to the extensive interactions that may be needed between executives or managers from your business and government leaders as you initiate or continue operations in their country. Certainly these interactions are a part of daily life for businesses in most of the world. In the modern industrial nations, especially the larger ones, such interactions will be more formal, structured, and similar to those in the U.S. In other words, they will be more bureaucratic, and will probably involve more bureaucratic functionaries. This is not the case in the bulk of the world's developing countries.

For countries that are not modern, the start-up of a sizable business operation by an enterprise from outside the country will occasion significant government involvement. In all but the giant less-developed countries such as China and India, where top-level contact is nearly impossible due to the very size of the countries, you will find that any significant new business proposal will bring with it the need and the opportunity to meet with relatively senior officials.

Such meetings might for the most part be with those below the cabinet level, but in many countries you may find yourself meeting directly with a senior official to push your project. This is, of course, more likely to happen if you are making a large investment or asking for a substantial favor such as favorable tax treatment or the use of local natural resources. Cabinet ministers responsible for areas such as trade, labor, finance, and industry are likely to be on your agenda, and in rare circumstances you may even meet with the head of state.

Needless to say, this is all an adventure, a great challenge, and pretty exciting, but in the end you are trying to get something started and you must remain focused. In your start-up visits as well as your ongoing operation, you must always have someone in your party able to meet with such officials. Basically, that person must be capable of polite, diplomatic discussion while clearly knowing the range of acceptable negotiating possibilities for your business and any applicable U.S. laws or policies.

I remember being in a distant country, waiting with an associate in that country's executive mansion for a session with its president. While I sat comfortably on a sofa in a hallway outside the meeting room in this very impressive home, the vice-president walked by and stopped to chat. In a few minutes we were ushered into a room to meet a living legend. He sat on one sofa, I on another, and a minister and my associate on a third. We talked about our business plans only tentatively, after a round of social niceties, comments about the president's background and interests, and so on. I can only say that meeting with a major leader in an exotic land halfway around the world can seem unreal. The first time it happens, you may feel as if you are in an adventure movie, and you may really have to force yourself to concentrate.

Another time I had a meeting with a top minister in an African country then in a horrible war. While we talked about business and political issues, just outside the city people were being shot as battles raged. It was simply bizarre, like being in a Kafka story.

Once in Saudi Arabia I was going to meet a top official in the remote summer capital of Taif, and I had carried a bottle of water in by briefcase (as a hedge against the arid heat). On passing through security, their reaction led me to believe that I might be spending the rest of my life there, short though it would surely be. Bottled water, it appeared, looked like nitroglycerin or some other explosive chemical.

There are endless such experiences awaiting you, and you will have them. You will be meeting with senior dignitaries if your business is of a significant size. The worlds of business and government blur in many nations.

From the perspective of the ongoing operation, if your business happens to be of strategic value to the national government, the manager of your local operation may be in frequent meetings with top officials, especially in the poorer nations. I recall a country in Africa that late every afternoon called the managers of local affiliates of important foreign firms for consultation on economic issues. The foreign general managers were very much valued as sources of information and advice for the government. In fact, such managers may find that their social circles frequently include senior government officials.

LOCAL GOVERNMENT OBJECTIVES MAY NOT BE YOUR OBJECTIVES

Whether the local government is involved in your business directly through some form of partnership or just through its oversight role, it is easy to understand that its objectives may not be the same as yours. In the developing nations especially, the government will likely be more interested in providing an adequate supply of inexpensive, essential products for its citizens than in maximizing your profits. If your particular case involves corrupt local politicians, the government's objective could be almost anything, and your operation may be continually at odds with the officials interacting with your business.

INTERNATIONAL GOVERNMENTS AND QUASI-GOVERNMENTS

Beyond the local government, your business may be influenced by international organizations such as the World Bank or the IMF. This is not all bad, for as discussed in Chapter 7, these groups generally support private enterprise and often unofficially will be on your side in discussions with the host government. Unfortunately, their staffs may at times convince the government of the need to pursue a project in your industry that in your view is not needed and that, more seriously, may require you to put up serious funds.

As noted, the various international aid groups may also get involved in your business by indirectly providing funding either to you or to your competitors.

THE U.S. GOVERNMENT ROLE

The host government is not the only one that may influence your operation in its country. The U.S. government, in its political objectives, may have a serious impact on your efforts. This may occur in modern areas such as Europe or Japan, or in highly undeveloped areas like Zaire. Certainly the economic and military might of the U.S. is a quiet, positive presence with you and your company whenever you deal in a foreign land; this power can indeed be beneficial if you are dealing with a difficult government that otherwise could undertake some action harmful to your business.

The other side of the U.S. government relationship is that the United States has definitely shown it will use its economic clout to support its political objectives. In the case of the Republic of South Africa, the U.S. was very active in setting up trade embargoes and establishing tax laws that in the end led to many American companies withdrawing from the country. Even governments of various U.S. states and cities were active in such legislation. China, with its human-rights issues, is always at risk of such action by Congress if not the administration, as are other nations. Needless to say, if your business is operating in a country that receives such treatment, you may not be very happy.

Another important area of U.S. government influence comes from the Foreign Corrupt Practices Act. This act, passed by Congress in 1977, applies to U.S. corporations operating around the world. It strictly prohibits American companies from making payments to foreign government officials, foreign political parties, or politicians seeking office, in order to gain or maintain business. Penalties for breaking this law include imprisonment and fines. Companies from other modern countries are not necessarily under such restrictions, as you likely will discover. I personally do not believe this to be a burden for American businesspeople. On the contrary, the law gives American businesspeople something to quote in tense situations; in fact, foreign officials are usually aware of it and it never needs to be mentioned.

Faced with companies who compete by disreputable means, Americans must be more creative. If their company is sufficiently large, perhaps as part of their entry negotiations with the country they can offer to support some key program in the country or local community, such as scholarships for local students or a medical program. The country would benefit, and perhaps the pertinent government official might see some benefit by association. Moreover, such a socially responsible act is indeed legal and positive, and makes for good public relations.

CONCLUSION

Governments of other lands are active players in their economies, some positively and some very negatively. You will encounter their involvement in two areas. First, your international competitors from other modern countries will likely be supported by their home governments in their efforts abroad to a far greater extent than you will be supported by the U.S. government. Second, within the country in which you are interested, you probably will find the involvement of the host government to be unlike that experienced at home. In some countries the government's interest will be refreshing and encouraging as it backs your business efforts; elsewhere it will be restrictive and even frightening.

12

Oops! Political Risks

There is no denying it: When you are engaged in business in another nation, you are working not only in another culture and society; you are also living and operating under other laws, regulations, and philosophies about government, business, individual rights, and much more. No longer are you or your business under the protection of the central, state, or local U.S. governments. To a very great extent, you are out there on your own. The laws and regulations that affect you are those of that land; the officials you deal with are those running that country.

In Chapter 11 we reviewed ways in which local governments may become involved in your operations. We have hinted about political risks; it's time to talk about those risks openly, beginning with an old bugaboo that is really not much of a threat today.

NATIONALIZATION

Nationalization is the seizing of a company's business and assets by the local government. It happened in Venezuela in 1976, when the government grabbed the assets of American oil companies. It happened in 1982 in Mexico to major commercial banks, which have just recently been sold back to the private sector. The current open climate in most of the world, with the steady progression to private enterprise and more open governments and societies, has greatly reduced the nationalization risk, and it should not be a great concern to you as you contemplate business abroad.

FINANCIAL PRESSURES

If indeed the country has insufficient hard currency to support all its needs, your business may suffer. Certainly any request to use valuable hard-currency funds to repatriate dividends will not be warmly received.

In a variation of this pressure, if a government or one of its entities has an equity interest in your business operation, it may press you to maximize dividends. This certainly will be the case for any government in desperate need of funds, whch includes most of those in the world. As noted in Chapter 7, if the country has minimal hard currency and your operation maximizes dividends, the government will be happy with its share; but your share paid out locally will languish in a local bank awaiting the needed hard currency for the conversion to send the dividends home. While in the bank, these dividends will suffer from whatever local inflation and devaluation takes place. In Moslem areas where interest is frowned upon, the funds may not earn any. In such an environment, you may prefer to withhold dividends and keep the funds invested in the business, where you can at least attempt to protect their real value. This may not, of course, be possible.

Other financial pressures may relate to the value of your products to the country. If your business is in an essential area such as energy, other valuable raw materials, or food, which have a wide customer audience in the country, a government having difficult financial times will undoubtedly press you to keep local prices down. This pressure can reach truly insane proportions, including the formal establishment of prices that are below your real costs. I know this sounds draconian and bizarre, but it is a real risk in economically deprived areas, especially if the host country is ruled by a despot who is lining his own pockets.

PERSONAL RISKS

This is a broad category, encompassing a range of risks. Aspects of crime, health, and the like that are not directly related to political pressure are covered in Chapter 13; here we are focusing only on political risks.

Consider a business in a developing country in which the government officials apply strong pressure to achieve their aims. An existing operation may be pressed to invest in a particular locale or project. In such circumstances, you should first counter with reasonable business arguments, then, if the pressure increases, try to move the discussion to other fronts. You might try to show that your business will have to shut down if forced to take such a step. You may attempt to present a united front with other companies in the industry if all are being similarly pressured. You could try to solicit the support of the U.S. embassy and trade organizations to press your case.

As an illustration, once a dictatorial government attempted to force an industry to sell products below cost, in effect driving the entire industry out of business. Because the products of this industry were essential to the country, the government sought to keep the companies working (albeit at a steadily increasing loss), to which the companies and their parent corporations responded by attempting to bring in any international organization that would help. Eventually the government relented.

In such situations the life of your manager can become very difficult, whether he is from outside the country or a local. If the country is potentially dangerous, as it may be in such a situation, the manager may want to get his family out. He may also find himself under arrest if he fails to obey the government. I have seen this occur for a top local manager of a foreign-owned business, and for a manager from outside the host country; both cases were in countries with autocratic governments.

Such pressure on you or your employees cannot be easily understood by those back in the happy confines of the U.S. It is particularly prevalent in less-developed nations that have not yet joined the development trail.

Having said that, I would note that polite threats can pop up anywhere. In Chapter 4, I told of being invited to the home of an individual who somehow was related to those in authority. During the course of the evening (and amid generally friendly conversation), my host described some trouble he had had with a foreign businessman. As I've said, he then mentioned how he could make a telephone call and instantly close the routes out of the country—the international airports—to anyone he chose. I leave it to you to decide if this was just a casual story.

CORRUPTION PRESSURE

Pressures of this nature will most likely occur in the less-developed countries, but not always. Let's look at a likely scenario. Suppose that you have located a country with potential that is developing, clearly growing from a poor economic base, and you believe it would be just the right country for you and your business. You do all the necessary investigative work at home and send a talented team to the country for research, perhaps even going yourself. In the course of this visit the team eventually determines the key persons that will be important in your company's entering and beginning operation. Perhaps you even secure the services of a good local counsel. During the visit or a subsequent one you meet with the appropriate officials to describe your plans, and are well received.

In succeeding weeks and months you and others locate good potential partners and you select one, a person who appears well connected and knowledgeable in the local market. This partner provides beneficial advice to the effort and attempts to make headway when you or others are not there. Days turn to weeks and weeks to months; you make more and more trips, and hold cordial meetings that get nowhere. Ideas are discussed that seem to be well received, but there are no quick replies.

Sometime in this effort you will eventually realize that nothing is going to happen unless you change your approach. The wrong people may be involved; perhaps you should have been consulting someone else. Perhaps you have committed some unwritten breach of etiquette, failing to consult first with some important, respected authority, official or not. (In one rapidly growing country I saw a facility that did not open for years because the developers failed to involve someone who had the clout to keep it closed.) There is also the possibility that you could come up with a more attractive entry plan, one more appealing to the country. All are possible explanations for the delay, and you should explore each.

Finally, there is the possibility that someone you are meeting with expects something more. That "something more" is never mentioned in conversation, and you have to figure it out. Of course, when you do figure it out, you will realize that you don't want to do business with this person, and unless you can find some other avenue, I suggest you look for another market. If you indeed encounter such a stumbling block, others in the country may support your entry; you then just have to find them. Nevertheless, if you refuse such an unspoken request (and I strongly recommend that you do), you must recognize that this may create a strong opponent in a very influential position. You must weigh each situation for itself, but this situation can stop you in your tracks. The person in question may even be very high in the country's government.

Political Risks from the U.S. Government

In Chapter 11 we reviewed areas of unexpected influence on your foreign operation from the U.S. government. I will not repeat them here other than to state again that unlike even some major European countries, the U.S. has demonstrated that it is very willing to use its economic might to accomplish political aims. The U.S. does not separate its economic interests from its political ones; this has been apparent in relations with Vietnam. Companies from France and Japan are actively seeking market positions there while those from America are restricted from such operations. The South Africa story recounted in the previous chapter is the best example of U.S. political priorities seriously damaging the interests of American companies in foreign lands.

Another aspect of such political risks is that of a reaction the host government may have to positions of the U.S. government. It may not be comfortable to work in an affiliate of an American company in a nation under political criticism from the U.S. That certainly has been the case in U.S. companies operating in various Middle East countries over the years, bringing valuable resources back to the U.S., but for the most part with employees and families who feel ill at ease as they live and work in a threatening environment. When the U.S. decides to press a foreign leader on issues such as human rights or democratic values, it can become unpleasant to work in that country. Several nations have come under such pressure, including South Africa, Zaire, China, and Chile.

CONCLUSION

When you become involved in the international world, you are two things. First, of course, you are a businessperson, operating internationally. Second, you are a representative of the United States, whether you want to be or not. You are an American and your operation is American, even if all the employees are local, and everything you do or say is viewed with that cast. There are great benefits to being American, but there can be great risks too. There are also political risks that have nothing to do with your nationality.

In any event, you will find the political and business worlds much more closely entwined abroad. This probably is not to the liking of most American businesspeople, who dearly love to avoid politicians, but it is a reality, and you can get used to it.

13

SECURITY:
THE BUSINESS,
THE EMPLOYEES,
AND YOU

You and those involved in your enterprise naturally bring with you your own cultural attitudes, professional experiences, and values but now you all must survive and prosper in another set of circumstances. There are questions to be addressed: Is the investment secure? Can it suddenly be taken away? Can you operate your business as you would like to? How safe are you, your employees, and their families? What other concerns imperil your living a healthy, satisfying, secure life? Is food available? Are there deadly or unfamiliar diseases? Are there political terrorist groups that might delight in taking American hostages?

It's a big list; fortunately, in most places the risks are no greater than they are back home. For example, many countries have lower rates of violent crime than does the U.S. In this chapter we will examine what you, your employees, and their families may have to put up with to be successful, and will look again at aspects of investment risks that have been covered in passing in the preceding chapters. Generally speaking, the twenty or so modern industrial countries will have security environments comparable to that of the U.S. The remaining 90 percent of the world's countries, which vary greatly in this respect, are the focus of this chapter.

INVESTMENT SECURITY

This is always a concern, although it seems to be of less significance than in earlier decades. As mentioned, nationalization is a way to lose everything, or at best to be compensated poorly for your assets. This takes place when the host government is moving away from private enterprise (which is extremely rare today), or when it is in a serious dispute with the government of your company's home country. This is always a possibility, as there are usually several countries unhappy with the United States who may decide to take such action.

If your business is nationalized, your recourse is primarily through the U.S. government. Depending on the circumstances, anything can happen, including reversal of the process, compensation, or nothing. Compensation, however, may take decades, and will undoubtedly be only a fraction of the real worth of your business. Certainly you should not enter any land where there is a significant risk of nationalization.

Another form of investment risk relates to the subject of Chapter 6. If you decide to close down the business, will you be able to bring your original investment home? The answer, briefly, is most likely yes for any operation in the modern industrial countries; however, this becomes increasingly remote the more undeveloped the country in question. There are real barriers that we have already discussed, such as the possibility that the host country may not have the hard currency for you to repatriate your investment, even if you are able to sell it locally to another investor. In such a case, the repatriation may have to take place over several years.

OPERATION SECURITY

As we have seen, the government in some lands may press to have one or more of their people in your employ. In lands with strong government involvement, moreover, your operation may be subject to price controls, currency controls, and more. The government will want to know a lot about your business, and you may find little privacy as a result.

We have also discussed how you may encounter pressure from the government through the partners you choose, who may themselves be in or closely connected to the government. In the less-developed countries, this may be obvious.

Regarding criminal problems, you will have to take the same steps you would in the U.S. to protect your offices, plants, and other facilities. In some poor countries, you may also need to train your staff in what behavior is expected and what is not, or what they can take home and what they should not.

COMMUNICATION

In countries with authoritarian governments you may quickly realize that your communications are probably not private. In poorer lands, telephone facilities are terrible. Even Brazil has relatively few telephones. Although not necessarily a barrier to business, having a telephone installed in Brazil costs $2,000, almost equivalent to the average annual income of a Brazilian.[1] That is why investment in the state telephone company might be an attractive risk for international equity buyers seeking privatization opportunities; the potential is great.

In many places, telephone availability is not enough to satisfy an American's desires. It may be impossible to have a telephone at home, for example, and even if it is there it may not work. This is not true in modern lands, of course, but it is in many others.

You will therefore need to develop reliable methods of communication with the home office and within the country. Facilities such as telexes are very valuable in countries with poor telephone capabilities. There are countries in which the managers of the local operation communicate by high-quality radios.

In one particularly poor nation, I recall seeing those desiring an international telephone call lining up hours in advance outside the central telephone office. Use of the telephones in the company facility was considered impossible. One manager worked steadily to build a warm relationship with the telephone operators in order to be able to receive priority treatment to make a call more quickly in an emergency.

Of course, there is also the language problem. In a non-English-speaking land, unless foreigners learn the language they are always in the dark and at increased risk. I recall the story of two good friends who lived in Japan. One particularly gray day the wife went out window shopping, unaware that the television and radio had broadcast typhoon warnings and urged all to take cover. She never bothered to listen to the television or radio because she couldn't speak the language.

It is a fallacy that English is the only language anyone needs anywhere in the world. This may be true in international airports and hotels, in major restaurants in capital or leading cities, and perhaps in dealing with senior officials and business leaders in some parts of the world. It is not true elsewhere. In the Middle East, my associates and I once got home from a totally Arab-speaking neighborhood only by having a picture of the building to which we wished to go. We could not even count on the taxi driver being able to read an address written in the local language, as he proved to be illiterate, and he surely did not recognize our pronunciation of the name of the building. The old axiom about English is another excuse Americans use to avoid learning other languages.

One of my old pastimes was to learn about a hundred words in each major language. People would ask if I spoke this language or that, and of course I never did, but I could get to the airport or the hotel, call the police, ask how much something cost, say a gracious hello and goodbye, and survive. I recommend learning a second language, or even a third. Spanish is certainly a top candidate for that second language, as it is widely spoken in so many developing countries, and so closely related to Portuguese and Italian. Others might be Mandarin or Cantonese, given the growing economic prominence of the Chinese world. Certainly there are many countries in which someone in your group had better speak the local language; it's either that or have a translator.

PEOPLE CONCERNS

This is what really counts. If your managers and staff and their families are not secure, there is little chance for a successful operation. Certainly personal security is not as serious a concern in the modern nations as elsewhere, but issues exist even there. If you bring in key people and their families from the outside, you had better pay attention to the area in which you expect them to live. Even in some modern nations, there are areas in which no one will speak English, where there may not be attractive schools for the American children, where Americans may not be liked, and where living conditions are difficult.

Knowing the Rules

Unless you have done a great deal of research, you can never know all the local rules, but you must nevertheless try to, both the official ones and the unwritten social ones. The company must take steps to ensure that its employees have training in this.

Not many years ago there was a popular story about an employee from the U.S. who flew to a major Middle Eastern nation on, I believe, a Friday afternoon. The following Monday, a colleague in the United States was speaking to another associate in that nation, and asked if the traveling employee had arrived and was busy working. The frightening reply was no, he had not been seen. A frantic search ensued; the airline confirmed the traveler had been on the flight. The staff in the Middle Eastern country could find nothing, not a clue. He was not at the scheduled hotel and had contacted no one. Using up all the goodwill chips the staff had earned over the years, the company pursued the matter through military and police channels. After a couple of more days, the American was located in a jail at the airport; he was apparently so excited about the trip and his assignment that he had taken pictures of the airport upon his arrival. This was specifically forbidden by the country, which considered the airport an important military location; as a result, he had a rude greeting. Furthermore, the jail didn't provide sustenance, so he wasn't in good condition. It was a simple mistake with big consequences.

Housing Security

People need to feel secure at home. In a strange land, your staff and their families will feel uneasy no matter how secure the surroundings. If the country is modern, or at least offers modern living conditions, the situation will not be so shocking, and perhaps some guidance is all that will be needed in finding accommodations. In other lands, the problem is more severe. In the poorer lands of Africa, Latin America, and Asia, for example, a foreign employee and his family may appear to be wealthier than the population at large, which is of course the case. Housing that will make this family happy will be beyond what the majority of the population can afford; as a result, you may even get into the business of supplying the housing. In the most difficult lands, companies have in the past provided compound housing, although this tends to be frowned upon by host countries, and companies seem to be moving away from it. It was nevertheless utilized throughout the Middle East in the past, and in some African lands. The benefit of compound housing is that security arrangements can be made for the entire compound. Families may also have others from their home country or from similar modern countries with whom to associate. A negative aspect of this is that the foreigners mix far less with the locals and learn less about the host country, in addition to sending an unintention signal to the local residents that the foreigners may not be interested in their culture, or may consider themselves above the local environment.

Crime is a serious threat in the poorer nations, and the need for secure housing is real and deserves careful consideration. The sources you pursue for other business information will also be able to give advice about where to live. Managers of other foreign-owned companies, the local U.S. embassy staff, members of the local branch of the American Chamber of Commerce, and similar groups are good sources of such information. The local counselor recommended throughout this book is another good source. The level of security required will of course have to be determined in the specific locale.

There are indeed a very few countries where Western-ers, and in particular Americans, may be at particular risk; again, these are nations engaged in disputes with the U.S. If you are involved in such a place, you must be concerned not only with simple crime but also political or terrorist crime. There are actually few countries in this category, but they will be pretty obvious; a couple of Latin American countries highly active in the drug trade would fit this cat-egory, for example.

Health Concerns

Perhaps greater than the issue of physical security against crime is that of health. This concern takes more than one form. There are indeed horrible diseases in some lands that do not exist in the U.S., and we will review a few. More common, however, is that anyone from outside the coun-try will have to adjust to the local standards of cleanliness and to the local bacteria. This does not purport to be a medical chapter, but a couple of simple examples will make this latter point. We are all familiar with jokes about "Montezuma's revenge" describing how visitors to Mex-ico had better be careful not to drink the water lest they get dysentery. Most of us know someone to whom this may have happened. Similarly, if we visit a very poor land in Africa or Asia, we should be very concerned about the cleanliness of the eating utensils, about drinking bottled water, and so on. Such precautions are helpful to a certain extent. Unfortunately, there is more to all this. People become acclimated to the bacteria in their environment. An American who gets dysentery in another land is not simply reacting to poor standards of cleanliness there; he is also reacting to new bacteria. Foreign visitors to the U.S.

get ill at times after eating our food or drinking our relatively clean water. Such experiences are common worldwide; I remember a meeting in an Asian country at which some participants from Africa became horribly ill. Again, it's a problem of acclimating oneself to another land and situation, even to local bacteria.

There are nevertheless serious cleanliness concerns in less-developed lands of Africa, Asia, and Latin America. When I first began working in such places, I gradually picked up some simple rules from listening to a variety of experts—some doctors, some just long-term survivors of tough areas. For one, I never drink the local water. There may be such countries in which you can eventually become acclimated, but the risk of infection is just too great, especially in poorer areas. If you are in a place in which there is no bottled water available, turn to other bottled drinks, for example soda and beer. In steamy, hot, difficult environments, there always seems to be a local beer, which in general is pretty good. I recall brushing my teeth on a tiny island in the Pacific with a soda one day; it wasn't bad, although it may have defeated the purpose of brushing in the first place. One caution is to avoid ice. Many people fall ill from having a drink poured over ice made from the water they've so carefully avoided.

Another simple rule is never to eat with utensils or a plate that are still wet. I know this is not necessarily sufficient, but I did decide I would be content when they were dry. It was a simple standard.

In some countries foreign residents will learn they must treat the vegetables they buy. In some cases not even boiling is a sufficient precaution, as they may have been grown with dangerous fertilizer. There are chemicals available for such purposes, but only in very poor lands are such precautions necessary.

Food fits right into this discussion. In the modern lands this becomes a delight; the foreigner gets to try endless new dishes. Eventually you may crave a hamburger or some ice cream if they are not readily available, but those you can fix for yourself. Even in poorer lands the dishes are exciting; the problem is the quality of the ingredients and their availability. Foreign residents learn how to seek out needed items, hoard key ingredients, and avoid eating certain things that are not worth the health risk. It's best to eat only meats that have been thoroughly cooked, never to eat fresh salads, and to eat fruit that you yourself peel. Salads in particular look healthy but are often a disaster, being washed in the local water and probably grown with questionable fertilizer.

Disease and medical treatment is the last big category of concern. You must ensure adequate medical care for those you bring into the country. In modern lands this entails establishing relations with the local medical community and advising employees on how to proceed. In other nations, your role will vary. Even in poor lands, in a major city there may be a quality hospital and good doctors, and this relationship can be arranged. In many of the poorest lands, however, there may be few if any skilled physicians, and no hospital at which you would want to be treated. In such a case, depending on the size of your business, you do the best you can, perhaps providing a company physician, and arrange to fly people out for serious problems. There is even a firm that flies people out on an emergency basis to get treatment in London and elsewhere.

Among the major diseases to be encountered, malaria is widely present in more than one form, and can be contracted in Africa, Asia, and Latin America. There is no absolute prevention or cure, but there are precautions, and anyone working, visiting, or living in these areas should be appropriately prepared. The usual practice is to take one of several medicines that either help fight off the disease or strengthen the person should he or she contract it. Quinine is in some of the medicine, but there are forms of malaria that require other treatments. The best advice is to get the latest information from the Centers for Disease Control in Atlanta (hot line (404) 332-4559 for international information), your local doctor, and especially from medical practitioners knowledgeable about the locale in question. The average American physician just does not have experience in dealing with such diseases. New York City has a hospital for tropical diseases, and medical centers in London and Paris seem to be especially knowledgeable, perhaps because those countries have been more involved for longer periods in these difficult areas of the world. There are sometimes medicines available in such European lands that have not yet been approved in the U.S.

There are numerous other bizarre diseases such as bilharzia (schistosomiasis), which can be caught by going into the fresh waters of Africa, as well as those in parts of South America, Asia, and southern Europe. The best step is to review the specific advice for the country in question from the Centers for Disease Control.

CONCLUSION

Try not to be frightened by the issues covered here. Thousands of Americans, Europeans, and Japanese travel through all the countries of the globe, exploring new opportunities, setting up new businesses, and having the time of their lives. You should be aware of these security and health concerns, but they should not deter you from pursuing your business goals. After all, Americans have become accustomed to a high level of violent crime, and in this area most nations are at least as safe as is the U.S.

14

ENVIRONMENTAL ISSUES WILL FOLLOW YOU ANYWHERE

Environmental requirements are a constant consideration in the minds of American business people as they go about their daily activities. This issue has grown from only sporadic consideration to one of primary attention whenever major investment or operating decisions are made. The federal, state, and local governments are all active in this field.

Although all businesspeople surely want a pleasant, clean world for their families and their descendants, they also know that discussions involving environmental concerns can become outrageously political, and that at times there seems not to be a rational trade-off of the factors involved, including environmental goals, economic productivity, and employment targets. Americans are like that; we seem to look at one goal at a time rather than consider them together to reach an appropriate balance.

The experience of years of trying to deal with environmental pressures while remaining competitive has given many American businesspeople something like a constant sour stomach about environmentalism. This history also leads to the risk that these same businesspeople will make a grievous error when looking internationally at business prospects. The thought may have crossed your mind, especially if you are involved in manufacturing: Other countries do not put all these stringent requirements on their companies. That's one of the reasons their products are at times more cost competitive.

But don't delude yourself into thinking that one of the benefits of setting up a foreign operation is the avoidance of environmental investments that would be required at home. It's just not true, certainly in the long-term picture. No business decision to go international should be made on the basis of avoiding environmental requirements. The entire world has bought into the environmental movement, although to varying extents depending on local circumstances. In this chapter we will look at that movement worldwide, the variety of situations and views that exist, and what your posture should be.

THE WORLD'S VIEW

What is the world's view toward environmental issues? Is the U.S. way out ahead in these issues, and the rest of the world basically asleep? The answer to the second question is a resounding no. Although there are those who argue that air and water quality are issues a society can focus on only after reaching a standard of living that satisfies more fundamental needs, the fact is that all the world is now well aware of major environmental issues. In June 1992, the United Nations held a meeting of leaders from throughout the world to discuss aspects of this subject.

It is true that the United States is in the vanguard of dealing with many of these issues, perhaps because our advanced industrial status made environmental problems most noticeable here first. (This might well be true for air quality in Los Angeles, for example.) Nevertheless, Europe is not far behind in environmentalism, if indeed it is behind at all. The leaders of the E.C. for environmental issues have stated a goal of making the E.C. the world leader in this area, and they are indeed very active. The Association of Southeast Asian Nations, ASEAN, has also been actively looking at environmental issues, although I would expect the economic interests in those nations to lead them toward economic development in the trade-off between development and environmental concerns. In the negotiations and subsequent political-insider battling over NAFTA, there was great pressure on the Mexican government regarding its environmental standards.

At this very point, the disparate viewpoints of the developed, industrialized world, and those of the developing world must be mentioned. While the modern industrialized world looked upon the United Nations conference as a chance to deal with major environmental issues such as global warming, it could be said that many in the developing world—and remember that this is the majority of the world—may have looked upon it as a session to focus more on development. The organization hosting the meeting was after all the United Nations Commission on Environment and Development.

There is indeed a basic conflict between the developed and developing worlds over just how tight world environmental standards can be. More than once developing-country spokespersons have remarked that they will not sacrifice their economic development in order to clean up world problems created by the industrial countries. The poorer of these developing countries have enormous problems, such as poverty and rapid population growth, that the developed world does not face to such an extent. In fact, there have been suggestions that the industrial countries might consider supporting environmental investments in the developing world, and steps have been taken in this direction.[1]

Despite the sharpened focus of developing nations on development, they are keenly aware of the possible costs of damaging their environments. Areas with wonderful tourism resources like Zimbabwe know they need to preserve their wildlife and natural beauty. Proud nations such as Nigeria are outraged when it becomes known that waste products from foreign countries are being dumped in their territory; they want the same high standards as modern nations have. There is always the question, however, of how much they can afford to lose, in both investments and jobs, due to tighter environmental controls.

Briefly, environmental restrictions will be tough throughout the industrial countries; the rapidly developing countries will be strengthening their controls (although mindful of the need not to harm their own growth); and the poorer nations will do what they can, possibly with funds from the industrial lands. After all, a million dollars spent on improving air quality at plants that have no environmental controls in a poor nation will likely have a far greater impact on the air of the planet than will spending the same money to further upgrade the already-advanced environmental emission-control equipment of plants in Germany or the U.S.

THE CURRENT WORLD ISSUES

There is an almost endless list of environmental concerns throughout the world, but as they realistically affect your business efforts, they might be summarized as follows:

- Air Quality. This simply means not putting harmful chemicals or particles into the air we all breathe.

- Water Quality. Again, this is a very obvious concern, and both existing and pending legislation is designed to clean up and protect the quality of the world's waterways. Raw sewage and industrial waste cannot be dumped into lakes or rivers without consequences to animal and human health, and world government and business leaders continue to seek solutions to this problem.

- Global Warming. This has been almost a war cry for many in the environmental movement; the theory is that due to the burning of fossil fuels in the past hundred years, the temperature of the world is gradually rising, with obvious dire consequences that could include the melting of the polar ice caps and the flooding of coastal cities such as New York. Most of the world believes this is a real problem, although there has been serious debate in the U.S. over the theory's validity.

- Sustainable Development. This may be the most relevant point for you. The majority of developing countries wish to see their economies improve as quickly and steadily as possible. Although such countries are interested in protecting their environment, they do not want to harm their own industrial development. The term "sustainable development" was used by the United Nations to refer to development that can be maintained without harming the prospects of future generations. What that rate actually is remains unknown, but whether the developing world would find it sufficient is highly debatable.

Many other issues deserve mention, such as land contamination, harmful chemicals in food, radiation risks, and more. Perhaps the most positive current step is the focus on prevention, so that disastrously expensive clean-up efforts never have to occur.

WHAT SHOULD YOU DO?

This is the question, is it not? Your role is not to solve the
environmental issues for the world, nor to resolve the
trade-offs between development and environmentalism.
Your role is to determine how you and your business can
best participate in the international business world. As you
consider a country, if your work will involve manufacturing or other activities that have environmental concerns,
you will of necessity first look at the host nation's environmental regulations. These you obviously must meet. If
your venture is in a modern industrial country, that country's own regulations plus those under consideration are
very likely close to the world standard.

Second, you should look to any large international
trade groups of which the nation is a part (such as ASEAN
for Malaysia, Singapore, or Thailand), and attempt to as-
certain what might be coming in new regulations that
would influence the country. The environmental ministry
of the country with which you are dealing should be able
to help in this look at the future.

Finally, if you are considering a less-developed country, you should look toward the current standards in the
U.S. and the E.C. that would apply to your project were it
being proposed for one of those countries. This will indicate the gap between currently applicable local restrictions and those that might someday be required should
the tightest world standards become applicable through
the United Nations. You and your company, with all the
relevant advisers, must then decide how much you want to
invest in your venture to meet environmental standards
that are higher than current local requirements. Your
decision on this matter will of course be influenced by the
actions of competitors and what is needed to keep your
company world competitive. It will also be influenced by
the state of development and the environmental debate in

the host country and the likelihood that it will move quickly to world environmental standards. Some people argue that a company should maintain its U.S. environmental standards everywhere it operates in the world. That is an admirable goal, but might result in some of the poorest countries losing essential products or services. Citizens in such poor countries may be economically unable to pay the higher prices companies would charge to recover their local investment if made to meet the higher environmental standards.

One last concern is that if this new business intends to export products to other areas of the world, you must ensure that the products meet the environmental regulations of the lands in which they will be sold.

Deciding how much to invest in nonrequired environmental safeguards as a precaution against future government requirements is tough, but not unlike many more decisions that you make all the time in business.

Eastern Europe and the Former Soviet Republics

This chapter is not complete without a warning as to the quality of facilities in the newly freed areas of Eastern Europe and the republics of the former Soviet Union. More and more we hear horror stories of industrial facilities in these areas that were constructed with no knowledge of or concern for environmental standards. If you are considering investing in an existing facility in this area, you most assuredly should invest first in expert environmental advice. The privatization bargains being offered in these areas may be tragedies for the buyer unless he is able to recognize potential environmental problems and adequately protect himself from future liability by deft drafting of the purchase agreement. Even if that can be accomplished, it's questionable whether the buyer can ever provide adequate future public-relations protection. My instinct says no. Certainly, environmental risks from past operations and design flaws are a bargaining chip for the potential buyer in seeking a lower price.

CONCLUSION

You cannot base a country entry analysis on avoiding environmentally related investments; this subject will follow you wherever you go. How much your company should invest will be a difficult judgment call, lying somewhere between current local requirements and the most stringent ones in the modern industrial world.

15

HINTS ON NEGOTIATING WITH FOREIGN GOVERNMENTS

Now you are ready to consider how to go about negotiating the entry deal. That means securing the needed approvals from the host government to allow you to enter, begin, and participate in business. From the purely commercial side, it includes the negotiations with your partner or local equity owners if necessary.

Dealing with a prospective partner, whether a true partner or an equity holder, was covered in Chapter 4, and in general is similar to such negotiations if you were developing a venture in the U.S. The one great difference that you should never forget is that the partner will be far more knowledgeable in local issues and policies, in how to get things done, and in who to contact for help. Regarding negotiating with foreign governments, though, there are several basic issues to address, and they are the subject of this chapter.

WHAT DO YOU AND YOUR COMPANY HAVE TO OFFER THE COUNTRY?

Why should the authorities permit you to enrich yourself in their land? Why should they give you the keys to their turf? Certainly they all know—both those from modern industrial lands and those in the poorest—that if you are interested, you expect to reap some significant benefit from the effort. They may not clearly understand why or what that is, but may wonder why they should give it to you.

Your sales effort in these negotiations will be to convince the relevant parties that your entry is a positive thing for the country. In modern industrial lands, you may not have to press the case so hard, as there is a more open acceptance of firms operating between countries; but even there you will have to obtain legal approvals, permits, work visas, and more, and some of the same thinking will crop up.

What do you have to offer, anyway? Here are some possibilities:

- Jobs. This is foremost in nearly all countries of the world. There are not many places in which employment considerations are not of interest to the leaders and citizens.

- Technology Transfer. If indeed your venture will lead to the training of a significant number of people, and this training indeed represents skills and technology the country does not have, this is an enormous incentive. Many countries openly express a desire for technology transfer in foreign investment and business activities in their lands; China, for example, is very concerned with this subject. If you are bringing such an offer, you have a real inducement to emphasize in discussions.

- Hard Currency. For the many developing countries that are short of this valuable item, the level of your investment in the country and the amount of hard currency flowing from export sales, if there are any, will be an important consideration. If your venture is to be engaged in the export market, be sure to point this out, and stress its beneficial impact on the country.

- Public Relations. If the time appears appropriate, you should emphasize how your company operates in the communities in which it does business, focusing on contributions and other positive involvement. You might offer a public or community-relations program if possible, such as a scholarship fund or support for youth teams. Approval is not going to be based on this item, but it can't hurt.

What Does the Country Have to Offer You?

You must believe the answer is "a lot," or you wouldn't be considering it. Nevertheless, it is helpful in developing negotiating strategy to prepare and review a clear list of the benefits the country offers, one agreed to by all relevant parties in your company and in the team negotiating the deal. In Chapter 4 we listed several more generally desirable qualities, so they will not be repeated in detail here. Generally, they are a stable government with a positive attitude toward private business enterprise and reassuring investment policies; a stable and strong financial structure; the availability of labor; and an attractive, open, and growing market. Your venture may also likely have more specific wants, such as the availability of a needed resource at attractive costs.

WHAT WOULD YOU LIKE TO RECEIVE?

Beyond the basic qualities noted here and in Chapter 4, what would you like to receive from the negotiations? If you are bringing a valuable business enterprise into another country, shouldn't the country in fact be seeking you? Shouldn't they perhaps be willing to offer some special benefits to assure that you will pick their nation? Indeed, this is what some of the more successful small countries in the world are doing. They actually compete for companies, and beat out their competition by their offers.

For example, a country may offer tax benefits, especially for a sizable enterprise. These could include a tax holiday for several years, low rates, or investment tax credits. Depending on the size of your venture and of the country, this possibility can vary greatly. A huge business undertaking in a smaller nation will likely receive more consideration than the same endeavor in a major European country. In any event, you should research the possibilities through your counsel in the country. You should then bring up these considerations at the appropriate time if they have not already been suggested by the government. That time is probably a meeting with a sufficiently high official in the financial or industrial ministry, but it is not during a formal diplomatic meeting with the president or a top minister, at least not the first time.

Another government offer could be assistance in bringing in needed expert talent without undue hassle by the department that covers immigration and work visas.

Another could relate to the use of natural resources. If this is important to the venture, you may have to explain how you plan to protect the environment and the people. Nevertheless, if you are bringing benefits to the country, you should expect fair and attractive treatment, and a good cost for the resource.

Assistance in obtaining local approvals for the location of your enterprise is another possibility, and is especially important if you are building a manufacturing or shipping facility.

Countries that actually court enterprises may give you a list of offered benefits even before you request them, especially if the proposed business is of a type they are seeking. You might expect such treatment in some Asian/ Pac Rim markets, but they are a bit unique. Those involved in negotiating on your behalf must research what the country has offered in the past and what it might offer, and then agree about what to pursue. Don't be shy; this is when much of the success of the venture is made or lost.

NEGOTIATING IN THE LOCAL CULTURE

I hope you are not tired of the "culture" subject; it is unfortunate if you are, for this issue will face you and your company every day of its existence in the host country. Negotiating is also affected by the local culture.

Each country will have its own idiosyncrasies, and you will no doubt prepare as much as possible. Again, outside advice from your counsel is important, as are comments from the U.S. embassy and from top managers of other foreign-owned firms in the country.

Americans are perhaps the straightest shooters in the world. Even though we think we are sly and crafty in structuring how we negotiate, the fact is that we come on straight and strong, and often lay out our entire deck of cards right from the outset: quick, strong, and visible; yes or no; take it or leave it.

Many foreign lands are much more diplomatic, more cautious, and more civilized, both the modern ones and the developing ones. Many work through relationships, and if you are a typical American company, you don't have any. Your team just wings in, does some quick research, then meets and formally makes its case, all in a few days. Some of your competitors may have people in the country building relationships and trust; we have a long way to go in understanding that. Some American firms move their top managers in foreign assignments every two or three years; whereas their competitors may leave them in place ten years. Guess who has the better relationships with key government officials?

Always assume the negotiation process will take more time than you had anticipated; it will.

Beyond the slower pace and the diplomatic niceties, there may also be clearly different approaches in style. Americans like to make an offer, hear the other side's offer, and then seek a middle ground. That approach will sink the ship in some lands. I recall one Middle Eastern country in which the negotiators for the other side continually took incredibly extreme positions. The Americans present always became exasperated and were in danger of giving away something they should not have. When confronted with such behavior, the appropriate response is simply "no." You can always walk out; that has been done with great success. You should never let the other side believe that the deal is absolutely essential to your company or to you personally.

In some places, just the fact that the negotiating team is not in its home country makes talks difficult. Authoritarian countries or very different cultures can bring implied pressure on team members that should not affect the negotiation, but nevertheless might. In such places, if the deal is big enough, you might consider inviting the government's team to meet yours back in the U.S., or perhaps in London, Paris, or some other neutral site, thereby taking the pressure off your negotiators.

Another good piece of advice is never to assume that those in the room speaking through translators do not understand your language. Negotiators have been fooled endless times by this tired ploy, but it seems always to work. Of course, that your counterpart is using a translator may not be a trick but just the result of his not having a sufficiently broad vocabulary.

It's also best not to become enchanted by local cultural niceties. Sophisticated old-world nations seem to have this effect on Americans, who must avoid being so charmed by the people on the other side that they lose their negotiating edge. In Germany, in an old village that had survived World War II relatively intact, I was once engaged in negotiating with a local manufacturing company. The other side was represented by the head of the company and his attorney. Both were older gentlemen who had been in the war and had all the mannerisms of aristocratic military leaders, but who also had a very real charm. One even wore a monocle, and the other constantly dragged one leg as he walked. They insisted we break for lunch as the negotiations dragged on, and we ate a true German feast that they had obviously had specially prepared for the occasion. Certainly the entertainment was well appreciated, but as we all slowly (and a bit sleepily) walked through the picturesque village square back to the negotiating room, I fortunately had the presence of mind to whisper in my lawyer's ear, "Don't let me sign anything this afternoon!"

Beyond such considerations, other aspects of negotiating in foreign lands are not so different from those of business negotiations in the United States. The team should not allow itself to be pressed to agree or disagree on the spot. It should periodically leave the negotiations to reconsider and to seek advice from home if need be.

CONCLUSION

If those involved in negotiating are prepared as advised in this book, the process is just another challenge in the development of your business entry. Unpreparedness invites your hosts to take you to the cleaners.

16

RELATIONSHIPS WITH THE PUBLIC, THE EMPLOYEES, THE GOVERNMENT, AND THE BUSINESS COMMUNITY

By this point you have probably discerned a very important truth: Nothing in your venture is more important than developing the correct relationship with key groups of people involved in your efforts. We have already devoted a couple of chapters to people issues, discussing cultural differences and similarities, and the challenge they will represent. We have looked in depth at challenges to your employees, those you bring from outside the country with their families, as well as local ones. We have also examined the unique role of government as it affects business around the globe. The business community is another group you must, of course, relate to.

This chapter will explore aspects of all these relationships as they might affect your business.

Public Relations

In the end, your business depends upon acceptance by the local community, in furnishing workers for your facility, in buying your products, or even in tolerating your presence. If you are in a place that is not accustomed to foreign businesses (or perhaps any significant business presence), you have your work cut out for you.

Even if you have located in a major industrial area, the problems may be different than those you're used to. Perhaps the level of union involvement in business is beyond anything you have experienced back home. Maybe local workers are not interested in your thoughts about how and when the job should be done, and prefer to work as they are accustomed to doing. Perhaps a modern industrial country hass a blend of capitalism and socialism that you did not anticipate. Australia is such a place, as is New Zealand.

These are some basic public-relations steps to pursue from the outset:

- Background Study. There is no excuse for not doing background research into the local customs before getting actively involved, and that includes research into the local work practices.

- Reliance on Local Employees. Early in your efforts you should seek to enlist experienced and wise local individuals who will give you insight to and communication with the community. This is not the aforementioned outside counsel, but rather employees of your organization. Any business effort will of necessity rely almost entirely on local citizens; you need one or more you can count on to tell you when your ideas will not work due to some local consideration, to tell you what the people in the community are thinking, and to give you suggestions as to how to improve your image and your relationship with the community.

As your project develops, you might wish to have such a wise and well-connected individual in a senior spot on your staff, maybe even as a community-relations manager; you may also be fortunate enough to find an individual who can provide this input and still fill one of your other positions. As your business grows, you will find a need to have people at all levels in the organization who trust the top manager and will offer communications and insights in this general area.

- Advertising. You cannot effectively advertise without understanding the host community. If your business depends on a successful marketing effort, you have to reach the customers. A modern country will no doubt have advertising agencies, but the less-developed ones may have only one or two, or perhaps none. This is not a book on advertising, but I do want to warn against those who believe that American television commercials and advertisements can be utilized unchanged in a foreign land. This may be possible, but you have to take into consideration the local culture, religious orientation, and consumer market, and you surely need to have your local confidants—as well as any outside local firm in which you may have confidence—review your advertising plans.

- Public-Relations Expenditures. Such expenditures may be especially beneficial in less-developed areas to build relationships. A wise step if the business is large enough is to fund something of interest to the community that the local government cannot afford. This may include youth activities, an athletic event, music programs, art activities and exhibits, scholarships, or other such programs. The key is to learn what is desired by the community, and that requires working with local leaders and listening to your own employees.

Most public-relations efforts will not be foremost in your mind during the early phases of the venture, but you do need to establish and maintain good community relations in a foreign land. In more modern lands, public-relations expenditures may have to be larger to be noticed, and this may be difficult in the early days. If the country is interested in building its cultural ties to the U.S., you might consider sponsoring a cultural event that goes to the U.S., although this is more in the nature of government relations.

- Essential Needs in Poor Countries. In terribly poor lands, you might consider supplying an essential need. If your business is located in such a place due to the availability of a local resource, it is possible that your modern operation will be located amid great poverty. Provision of food or medical equipment would be a real community service, for example.

EMPLOYEE RELATIONS

This is a tired subject, well known in American business. I maintain it is of even greater import in a foreign land than it is in the U.S., where it should be a significant function. In the U.S., this tends to be what the company wants to do *to* the employees rather than together *with* the employees. In a foreign land, this had better not be the case. It should not be the case in the U.S. either, and one day American business will learn that.

A few suggestions:

- Respect. You knew this was coming; we've discussed it before. One sure way to start on the wrong foot is to disrespect your workers, their families, or their traditions. You are on their turf and are depending on their efforts. They indeed may not know your standards or customs, but they can learn, and if it becomes clear to them that you have their best interests at heart, you will have a congenial situation. If you are in a society that seems to have castes, whether formal or informal, and the mass of people fall into a lower, almost invisible caste, you cannot let yourself operate amid the aristocrats to the disdain of the others. Of course, you must function in the existing culture and structure and somehow relate to all. But remember that you are an American. One of the great international images of the U.S. is as a land of promise for all. Local people, especially the educated ones, already know something of the American myth, and you can hide behind it. Americans treat everyone the same, and you can show that to the employees. You, after all, are clearly not a member of the local culture.

- Understanding. We have discussed differences among people, for example that local citizens may not get as much to eat each day as Americans. If nutrition is sufficiently poor, they will not have the same energy level as you and your colleagues from home. There are several countries in the world in which the people appear weak and slow by our standards, due to malnutrition.

  We also have dealt with nonphysical differences such as religious traditions. If a people expect to pray every day at certain times, you had better allow for that. If you try to stop it, you might consider going home. This is another instance in which you need the advice of experienced locals on your staff.

- Employee-Relations Manager. This person should no doubt be a local, and one with sufficient background education that he or she can relate both to the local citizens and to the top manager of the business and his goals. The employee-relations manager should be one of the top manager's trusted confidants, able to communicate quietly with the employees, to hear their concerns, and to convey the management's concerns. You may not find such a valuable person quickly.

- Local Laws and Policies. Of course, the business will have to comply with local labor regulations. The employee-relations manager will have to work with government officials, and may need to go through your legal counsel or another government contact if this is not the manager's area of expertise.

GOVERNMENT RELATIONS

This area is close to my heart, as you have no doubt detected. Chapters 11 and 12 in particular focused on the unique aspects of government in the business world in many countries. You cannot afford not to have good relations with the applicable governments. The term "good" here does not necessarily mean happy and friendly; it just means honest, clear, cordial, and informative. You need to know when a government may take action that affects your business. You need to head off confusion before it begins. In a large, modern, industrial country such as those in Western Europe, government relations may mainly involve staying abreast of breaking developments, with little opportunity to affect such events unless your business is very large. Nevertheless, you need to know what is happening. In developing countries this relationship is crucial, as governments may at times consider steps that will have inadvertent but serious impacts on your business.

This is a tender subject. You want to keep government interference at bay, outside of your operation to the greatest extent possible. Nevertheless, you do want officials to trust your top managers, to believe what your company has to say, and to understand enough of the operation that they do not think of you as a potential cash cow for the country.

These are some points to consider:

- Government-Relations Contact. Note that the title here is contact, not manager. It is not necessary for the local operation to have a formal government-relations manager, and this function may actually be more successful if it is not formal and the relevant individual is not so prominently labeled. The point is that there must be someone in the local operation who knows who in the government to approach for answers, who hears of relevant government action while it can still be modified, and who is considered a trustworthy contact or friend by someone in government. The most appropriate person may be the senior employee on your local staff, assuming he has the skills. Ideally he will know your business and your goals. If the top manager can speak the local language well and is in the country long enough, he may eventually become the senior government contact himself, even if he is from outside the country; nevertheless, the need would remain for a smooth, knowledgeable, trusted local employee to work with the appropriate government people. In any event the top manager will periodically have to pay calls on senior officials, and may socialize with them from time to time.

- Don't Get Involved in Politics. This is the great admonition for business in a strange land. You won't understand all that is happening, even in modern countries. Stick to your business, try not to get associated directly with a particular political leader or party, and maintain workable relations with the government, whoever runs it.

- Always Be Aboveboard. Don't ever forget the Foreign Corrupt Practices Act. Remember, you can always hide behind the fact that you are an American or are representing an American company.

RELATIONS WITH THE LOCAL BUSINESS COMMUNITY

Whether your business depends on selling into the local market or is involved in manufacture for export, your presence will affect the local business community. In large, modern lands this may be minimal, but in smaller ones your presence may raise the wage level, may drain skilled talent, and may pressure other businesses to offer more benefits to their employees. Obviously, you want to avoid unpleasant challenges from the business community, although they are probably not your primary concern.

Marketing

If you are selling to customers in the country, you will have to adapt your techniques to the local market. This is not mysterious, but if you are the only firm from outside the country, expect some grousing. If you are very successful, expect a lot of it. In a smaller country where some of the competitors may be associated with the government, you may also receive some indirect pressure.

Manufacturing

Again, your behavior may affect the local labor market. In your entry efforts you should survey that market for appropriate wage scales, employee benefits, and the like. In the end you will have to offer what you believe necessary to attract the employees you want, and for that matter your company may have standards that it enforces everywhere it does business. Fair treatment of employees, regardless of what group they come from, is ideally one such standard.

CONCLUSION

Good relations with people in all categories is crucial to your success. You want your business to appear a positive, beneficial force in the life of the country—to the government, to the public, to your employees, and to the business community. At the same time you want to guard against the image of being a moneybag from the U.S. Ideally, you should seek to enter and begin operations without creating a ripple, blending right into society. It's a delicate role, but one that deserves great attention as you make your entry plans and take the initial steps to realize them.

17

Danger Signs: Head for the Door!

The world has abundant new business opportunities today. In exploring them and undertaking those that appear most attractive, you expect to encounter an array of difficulties; after all, business in the U.S. is accompanied by problems as well. Nevertheless, your background no doubt gives you the confidence that by hard work you can overcome enough of the problems to make your ventures a success.

You are right in expecting any effort to be accompanied by an assortment of challenges. Sometimes, though, the challenges are too demanding, or out of the ordinary; in other words, they represent real danger signs.

There are too many good opportunities out there to throw away your time and your company's future attempting to overcome obstacles that may eventually prove to be unsolvable themselves, or that are indicators to future serious difficulties. Americans are proud of their tendency to persevere, to work through difficulties and conquer obstacles, and certainly this is a great attribute. Undue perseverance against some of the danger signs discussed here, however, may just result in excessive pain and expense, without bringing success. Many of these you may be able to surmount, depending on the circumstances; sometimes that will not be the case.

If you encounter enough particularly threatening things early in the negotiations or start-up efforts, head for the door. Again, too many good prospects are available to enter one intentionally about which you receive early warnings.

DANGER SIGNS

Here are warnings of possible significant trouble. Taken together, they compose a checklist of danger signs that you should not ignore.

Extraordinary Government Staffing Demands

Starting up a sizable business in many countries may force you to deal with requirements regarding the use of local citizens in the operation. You will likely confront this almost everywhere, and can usually solve it by sincere negotiation with the relevant government parties.

The authorities may require that your business be staffed entirely by local citizens, or perhaps almost entirely so. Whether this is a problem depends on the sophistication of the local labor pool and the degree of complexity in operating your business. If you are developing a technically complex facility in a poor, largely undeveloped country, such staffing requirements can pose a real problem, and will entail your working out a balance with the government among training you will provide, the actual number of locals you are required to hire, and permission to have enough of your own expert talent on hand so that the endeavor does not quickly collapse. I have met with government authorities who were absolutely unyielding about having a huge majority of locals in a new, technically complex facility. The negotiations were tense and difficult, but eventually the situation was resolved much along these lines. If the government never bends, and you cannot see how to safely begin operation, you can't. Chapter 10 offered insights on how to deal with this type of governmental requirement.

Another variant of this may be a requirement to put some political figure, perhaps a former politician or a current government bureaucrat, on your payroll as a senior manager. You may be able to live with this situation, and if you can develop a good relationship with the person, his contacts and influence may prove invaluable. He surely will be someone inside your operation with a direct channel to the outside.Then again, he may be an incredible thorn in your side, demanding authority and perks without understanding the business.

Excessive Foot-Dragging by Approving Authorities

Covered in detail in Chapter 12, this is a sign that either you have approached the situation incorrectly from a political standpoint or that the authorities are waiting for something more. If that something more is bribery, you may be out of luck.

Inability to Meet with the "Right" People

Related to the point just mentioned, you may find it impossible to get in to see the right authorities; as a result, your venture efforts fail to move forward. Possible explanations are the same, as well. Very similar is the inability to learn what the entry requirements are or what you should do.

Implied Personal Threats

These are most likely to occur in an authoritarian regime. If you encounter threats of this type from influential people in the government, it is time to say goodbye to this country.

Excessive Government Controls on Business

If you discover that the government exerts controls on product pricing or on other aspects of business, you may want to stop the investigation at this point. The absolutely worst such case is that of the government exerting control over your product prices while the prices of your raw materials float with world-market levels.

No Assurance of Hard Currency Availability

If you are interested in a country that has soft currency, and if your efforts in dealing with the central bank and other financial authorities have not resulted in any assurances regarding your ability to obtain hard currency to pay for needed imports or to remit profits, you would be wrongly advised to proceed in start-up efforts. If you can't get positive words now, you surely won't get them later when you are, in effect, trapped in the country.

Tough Restrictions on Repatriation of Dividends

Aside from not having needed hard currency available, a country may actually have a regulation prohibiting the amount of dividends that can be repatriated, as discussed in Chapter 6. If the country is discovered to have such restrictions, you should probably stop the investigation. Regulations may allow no more that 50 or 25 percent of after-tax profits to be repatriated; indeed, in countries with difficult financial conditions, no remission at all may be possible. Even if such a country offers your business a guarantee that it can repatriate, you should look askance at such a statement. This dividend restriction is not a good indication of a beneficial working relationship.

Excessive Difficulty in Obtaining Visas

You will need to bring into the country business and technical experts as you and your company evaluate the possible venture. Extraordinary difficulties associated with entry or exit visa approval should give you pause. Even so, some countries that companies have found highly attractive for business can be exasperating in this area, so you may decide that the difficulty is not sufficient to deter your interest. Middle Eastern countries can be frustrating, for example, but the opportunities may be so great that you will be willing to put up with these irritations. I recall the case of a person stationed in a Middle Eastern country who learned that his daughter back in the states had died. His associates had to go to great lengths to get an exit visa for him and his wife so that they could attend the funeral, and even that required a couple of days. Is your business attractive enough to justify putting people under that type of nightmarish bureaucratic

control and stress? Do you have people right for that type
of situation?

No Applicable Laws, Regulations,
or Policies in Your Industry

In your investigation efforts, you may discover that the
country has no policies or requirements covering what
you intend to do. This is likely to occur in a less-
developed, poor land that has not had to deal with your
type of proposal before. For instance, if your company is
involved in the energy-exploration field, or perhaps in
some aspect of mineral mining, the country may have no
applicable regulations. This is not a reason for stopping,
but it should raise questions. For example, how will your
operation be overseen by the government? What might
the government do regarding taxes and other requirements that are not now known?

The goal is to try to resolve these issues before beginning the venture. In such a case, you may even get involved in recommending policies for the government
to consider. Certainly you should not proceed without
some clear agreement about how the relevant business/
government interfaces will be treated.

Local-Ownership Requirement

Many countries will have a requirement that a foreign venture have a local-ownership component. This requirement
in itself should not discourage you from engaging in a venture, although Americans do like to own it all. There is a
great benefit in having good connections to the local system and culture, as has been noted throughout this book,
and partial local ownership may help bring this about.

The real issues are who has the local ownership as discussed in Chapter 4, and who has operational control. This latter point is crucial, and you should think for a long time before giving that up, unless you are in a franchise-marketing business. Frankly, I don't think you should ever give it up.

You should beware that local partners may not be all that you think they are in the early negotiations. If the prospective partners do not know your business thoroughly, they cannot portray the depth of their strengths and contacts as you would expect. They may be totally honest, but you still might be misled into believing they have more to bring to the venture than is the case.

Unstable Political or Social Environment

Is the country likely to be engulfed in a civil war in the near future? Are significant groups within the nation interested in stirring up life there, in making dramatic changes? Even if you cannot identify any such groups, what is your appraisal of the quality of life and the opinions of the populace regarding their future?

There are very few places I have been where I truly felt uncomfortable. Many countries naturally do not have all the comforts of the United States, but you will find that those comforts really don't mean much. People are happy in Zimbabwe, on the island of Pohnpei in the Pacific, in Saudi Arabia, in Mexico, and so on. None of these countries has the standard of living of the United States, but they have much to offer and happy people.

Nevertheless, when I walked the streets of Monrovia in Liberia, for example, or stayed at the Hotel Africa, there was a heaviness in the air itself. One could tell that this was not a safe or happy place. Something dangerous could happen at any time, and a person of average sensitivity did not need to speak to a government official to know it. Of course, the society has since been broken apart by factional civil war, with much loss of life.

Don't ever make a decision about a country without yourself being there, walking around among the people, talking with leaders as well as ordinary citizens. The feel of a country, a city, or a people is unquantifiable but highly important to your final decision.

Overabundance of Competitors in an Attractive Market

We haven't discussed this point much, because the number of competitors is an issue you face in any business-marketing decision and is not unique to operating abroad. It is included here as a reminder that if you are considering a nation because of its market attractiveness, many international competitors may have made the same assessment, and there may be several strong competitors there or on the way. Surely Singapore is well known by now as a bright business star, and many companies around the world will consider it—as well they should—not just as a local market but also as a center of operation within its area. You should too, but be aware that you will not be alone. Of course, that everyone knows a place is good to do business does not render it unattractive. A rapidly growing market can tolerate many competitors.

A company once worked long and hard to enter an attractive country that clearly had an overabundance of competitors in its particular industry. The country was attractive, but the industry was not growing rapidly and there was simply no room; the effort eventually was canceled. The same thing happens daily in the U.S. whenever a company tries to enter a market already overburdened with competitors.

Attitude of Your Own Company Management and Staff

Not to be overlooked is the attitude of the management and staff of your own company. There must be strong support among management to undertake any international effort, especially if a company has minimal or no past involvement overseas. This entire effort is more involved than moving a business from Kansas to Iowa, and there will be hurdles to overcome. Naturally there will be those who do not agree with the plan; there must be sufficient support, however, that the venture is given an honest chance to succeed.

Second, the staff involved must themselves feel positively about the effort. This includes those that will be involved in investigating, start-up, and permanent assignment to the foreign land, as well as those in the home office that will support the venture, visit periodically, and interpret for other management. Chapter 10 discussed staffing issues in detail.

WHEN TO GIVE UP AND HEAD FOR THE DOOR

In your investigation and your entry efforts, you and your business will encounter many challenges, including some of those just listed. Certainly, you will not immediately head for the door but will, if there is any merit to your plans, attempt to resolve the problems. Nevertheless, the points listed raise very specific decision areas; these are deal-breaker issues. If you use all your business talents, make all the contacts you can, try all possible solutions, and still are faced with some of these problems, you had better think about packing your bags. Why knowingly leap off a cliff? Perseverance is both a virtue and a vice, and hanging around after the evidence is hitting you in the face is neither virtuous, admirable, nor profitable.

The experiences you have during your investigation, and particularly in the negotiation and start-up phases, are good indications of what you can expect if and when your business is operating in the country. There should be enough such warnings and ample time for you to avoid getting into a disaster.

CONCLUSION

The world is loaded with exciting opportunities and with countries and governments eager to work with you. There are just too many good opportunities to get involved in one which from the outset is clearly troublesome.

18

SO WHAT ARE YOU WAITING FOR?

Someday, sometime, if you are going to be successful in business, you have to start. It is indeed a shrinking international business world, one in which economic realities are far ahead of political structures. Whereas the modern industrial countries of Western Europe, the United States, Canada, Japan, Australia, and New Zealand are stuck in slow economic growth rates, many newly developing industrialized countries are growing rapidly. At last, "developing" aptly fits many of these lands.

Asia and the Pacific Rim clearly lead the rest of the developing world in economic progress; indeed, some nations will soon have to be considered part of the developed world because their economies are so strong. They are about to be joined by select countries elsewhere, including a few in Latin America. Mexico, Chile, and Argentina in particular are doing all they can to move into this group of attractive developing countries. They are struggling to correct past mistakes, busily privatizing

219

companies, and opening the way for private enterprise to prosper. Although Chile is surely ahead, all three seem to be well on the way. In Europe, Portugal and Spain should benefit greatly from the new economic order, while in Eastern Europe three countries in particular are trying to join in the climb: Poland, Hungary, and the Czech Republic have some real possibilities. So does the former East Germany, of course, itself now solidly a part of reunited Germany, which, though reeling from the costs of this absorption, will likely be a revived powerhouse by the end of the century. The newly free Eastern European countries seem to be ahead of the various former Soviet republics in their movement into the world of private enterprise. The former Soviet republics are trying, new ideas and initiatives are flowing, and they too represent opportunities, although in a much longer-range perspective.

For Americans and their companies to thrive economically (as well as culturally and socially) in this new world, American businesses must get more involved. Japanese companies seem to understand this and are everywhere looking for opportunities. Some American companies understand too, but not enough of them, and most assuredly not enough of the middle-sized and smaller American companies that could prosper through international operations.

Only a little more than 10 percent of the world's nations are modern industrialized countries. The rest of the approximately two hundred countries are developing, with a few of these still relatively inactive. Although opportunities remain in the modern 10 percent, the great, fast-growth opportunities are in the developing world.

In this book we have examined this world, and in particular its countries and markets. We have then considered many things unique to international business, from cultural differences to issues of international finance that are so extraordinarily challenging. We have seen how profits earned in a strange currency may not be worth anything if they cannot be exchanged for dollars, or if they cannot be remitted to the home office due to local restrictions. We have seen that there are numerous international development banks and other institutions designed to focus specifically on the development of these burgeoning countries, and that business people can be aided by these institutions.

We have noted that the competition may be drastically different, that government may be involved in ways we would never expect with our American background, and that companies from other modern countries may not follow the same rules as those from America, which are bound by laws of the U.S. government. We have also seen how this unique role of foreign governments—as well as the behavior of officials at the national, state, and local levels here—may bring unusual risks to those in foreign business.

Nevertheless, there are many unique opportunities, so attractive that many are willing to put up with difficulties. There are also extraordinary considerations regarding the human side of business operations, the staff and their families, that complicate the entire effort but that can be solved with forethought and preparation.

Then there are security considerations. Americans abroad live under the laws and policies of the land in which they are involved. They must work, thrive, and survive under those policies. For the most part, this is not an undue burden and is actually part of the enjoyment of the international effort, although special consideration in some areas must be given to health and food considerations, and sometimes to physical security.

Environmental considerations, we have seen, do not disappear when one leaves the U.S. shores, even if the country is in the developing world. Nevertheless, they are different. Although most nations seem to have recognized the importance of the environmental movement, the bulk of the world, which is made up of developing countries, keeps a strong focus on that very term, development. You must be aware of the necessity of meeting not only current but—more importantly—future environmental requirements, as you get involved in business around the globe.

In the last chapter we looked specifically at warnings, danger signs that should clearly and immediately indicate that a proposed business venture should not be pursued in a given country. These warning signs should enable you to avoid terrible business and personal costs in both money, time, and effort, but they should not frighten you unduly. Business always has an aspect of uncertainty, and by being alert to these signs, you can remove some of the greater risks.

By now you should be chomping at the bit, eager to jump out of your seat in that commuter railroad car, airplane, office, or perhaps den, and get going. That is my message: Get going!

The advice is to do your homework. As noted earlier, a little homework avoids a lot of grief. The Appendix gives a list of sources—and leads to others—that will enable you to do some of that needed research and get on with your involvement in the international business world. It even includes a section giving specific guidance for the smallest of businesses.

There is no great secret about why many Asian countries are doing so well: Asians are very hard workers, and they are working toward a generally comprehensive objective. They have bought into a program of economic development through a private-sector approach to business. Well, Americans work hard too, and private enterprise built this country. There is no reason why Americans cannot participate in these booming new areas and obtain a meaningful share of the growing international business world. Some firms have started, but by no means enough.

Get going! It's your future.

Appendix:
Whom to Contact
for Information

I. OVERVIEW

The following sections list the addresses and telephone numbers of valuable contacts. Many of the major institutions noted have been described in the text, so those comments are not repeated here. Notes are given, however, regarding the specifics of gaining information. These are by no means all the available contacts, but they should get you well on your way. You will find people at most of these locations eager to help, so just ask. Also given are suggested resource materials of immediate value, those that will save you considerable time. Section VIII gives a step-by-step guide for the smallest of businesses in their efforts to enter the international business world.

II. U.S. GOVERNMENT CONTACTS

There is an almost endless list of groups within the federal government that might have information to offer. Some major ones are listed here. You should at the outset request a copy of the pamphlet *Export Programs: A Business Directory of U.S. Government Resources,* which includes an extensive list of many such groups and gives information as to how to contact them.

Department of State

2201 C Street NW
Washington, DC 20525
Telephone: (202) 647-4000

This is a valuable resource. Through the general telephone number, you can be put in touch with the appropriate contact for your country of interest. Initially, you should ask to speak to the desk officer for the country. Depending on the size of your planned venture and your questions, you might be directed to others, including higher officials, such as area directors, deputy assistant secretaries, or eventually the assistant secretary for the region, such as for Africa or Europe. The desk officer will be able to tell you of the current state of political affairs, any hot issues between the U.S. and the other country, and may communicate to the U.S. embassy in the country to arrange a meeting for you with the embassy. The officer is also a good source for other leads.

Department of Commerce

Fourteenth Street and Constitution Avenue NW
Washington, DC 20230
Telephone: (202) 482-2000

Again, this is a good source. In particular, the Commerce Department is involved in various trade programs, and the secretary of commerce currently chairs the Trade Promotion Coordinating Committee, which brings together nineteen federal agencies to coordinate their trade-promotion efforts. This committee has established the Trade Information Center, whose purpose is to furnish information to businesses. Its toll-free number is (800) 872-8723.

International Trade Administration (ITA)

(in Commerce building)
Telephone: (202) 482-2000

Within the Department of Commerce is the ITA, which in general seeks to aid exporters. As part of this overall effort in the department and the ITA, there is a network of market specialists known as U.S. and Foreign Commercial Service specialists. They are located in district offices of the department in the United States and in foreign embassies. Calling (800) USA-TRADE will get you the location of the nearest district office.

In the Department of Commerce are also located desk officers specializing in trade and economic aspects of specific countries. They are known as International Economic Policy (IEP) country desk officers and can be reached by calling (202) 482-3022.

There are also trade specialists for specific industries who can be reached at (202) 482-1461.

Also available from the department is a quick update by fax on the economic and political situation in many countries in the world. By calling these numbers and following the instructions, you can receive by fax extensive and timely information:

Africa, Middle East, South Asia	(202) 482-1064
Canada	(202) 482-3101
Central Asia/Russia/Ukraine	(202) 482-3145
Eastern Europe	(202) 482-5745
Mexico	(202) 482-4464
Pacific Rim	(202) 482-3646

Office of Export Trading Company Affairs

(in Commerce building)
Telephone: (202) 482-5131

Among many activities, the office gives counseling to businesses regarding the export-intermediary industry.

Small Business Administration

408 Third Street SW
Washington, DC 20416
Telephone: (202) 205-6740 general
　　　　　(202) 205-6720 for Office of
　　　　　International Trade

The Office of International Trade works to assist small businesses in getting involved in exporting. It operates the Export Information System, which provides information on products in top world markets.

Export–Import Bank of the United States

811 Vermont Avenue NW
Washington, D.C. 20571
Telephone: (202) 622-9823

A great deal of information regarding the various programs of the bank can be obtained from its office of public affairs at (202) 566-8990. In addition, the bank has established a toll-free hotline for small businesses to contact, (800) 424-5201. Information will be given on a variety of issues, including availability of loans to finance sales abroad and export-credit insurance and guarantees.

The bank conducts seminars for businesspeople considering or already in the export market, from a one-day overview to an extensive four-day program. Information and registration can be obtained by calling (202) 566-4490.

U.S. Agency for International Development (USAID)

2201 C Street NW
Washington, DC 20523
Telephone: (202) 647-4000 general
                (800) 872-4348 or
                (202) 663-2660 for the Center for Trade and
                Investment Services
Fax: (202) 663-2670 for the center.

You may be able to supply USAID funded needs in some countries. USAID also may be able to lead you to further contacts in a particular country.

Office of the United States Trade Representative

600 Seventeenth Street NW
Washington, DC 20506
Telephone: (202) 395-3000

This is a good source for the status of any current trade talks between the U.S. and the country in question. This office also deals with unfair trade practices.

Overseas Private Investment Corporation (OPIC)

1100 New York Avenue NW
Washington, DC 20527
Telephone: (202) 336-8799 for materials and questions;
                (202) 336-8400 general number
Fax: (202) 331-4234

Centers for Disease Control

1600 Clifton Road
Atlanta, GA 30333
Telephone: (404) 332-4559

This telephone number is an international traveler's hotline. By using it, you can secure information on recommended immunizations and other health precautions before traveling to or taking up residence in a specific foreign country.

III. INTERNATIONAL DEVELOPMENT BANKS AND ORGANIZATIONS

Following are banks or organizations active in international development.

World Bank

1818 H Street NW
Washington, DC 20433
Telephone: (202) 477-1234
Fax: (202) 477-6391

The bank has offices throughout the world, but the Washington office is the world headquarters. There are an enormous number of employees. A call to the general number should lead to people involved in your particular country of interest.

The bank offers a series of monthly business briefings. These are one-day affairs; information on them can be obtained through external affairs, at (202) 473-1819.

The World Bank also turns out a wealth of publications, many summarizing studies conducted on specific countries. A wise first step might be to ask for the *Index of Publications* and the *Guide to International Business Opportunities*. Contacts for publications should be made at:

World Bank Publications
1818 H Street NW
Washington, DC 20433
Telephone: (202) 473-1155
Fax: (202) 676-0581

The bank also publishes an *International Business Opportunities Service,* to which you can subscribe by contacting World Bank Publications at Room T8094 at the above address, or by calling (202) 473-1964 or fax to (202) 676-0635. The publications of this organization are extensive. Once in touch, you will be able to decide if their publications are for your company or not. Another subscriber service, *Development Business,* can be obtained by calling (212) 963-5850.

There is also a contact for the World Bank in the U.S. Department of Commerce, should you wish to learn more about the bank before contacting it directly; that contact may be reached at (202) 482-4160.

International Finance Corporation (IFC)

1818 H Street NW
Room I 9163
Washington, DC 20433
Telephone: (202) 477-1234 general
                (202) 473-9119 for corporate relations
Fax: (202) 676-0365

The IFC is an institution within the World Bank group that provides support to the private sector in its efforts to promote growth in developing countries. It actually invests in commercial enterprises. You should contact the corporate relations unit to make proposals or obtain information.

Multilateral Investment Guarantee Agency (MIGA)

1818 H Street NW
Room H 6083
Washington, DC 20433
Telephone: (202) 473-6168
Fax: (202) 477-9886

MIGA provides guarantees against loss from noncommercial risks in foreign investment.

International Monetary Fund (IMF)

700 Nineteenth Street NW
Washington, DC 20431
Telephone: (202) 623-7000

Depending upon how much you want to know about the financial stability and performance of countries and their economies, you may want to explore the many publications of the International Monetary Fund. In particular, the monthly magazine accompanied by an annual yearbook, entitled *International Financial Statistics,* contains a wealth of economic data difficult to come by elsewhere. Information on IMF publications can be received and actual orders made at this address:

Publication Services
International Monetary Fund
700 19th Street NW
Washington, DC 20431
Telephone: (202) 623-7430
Fax: (202) 623-7201

Inter-American Development Bank

1300 New York Avenue NW
Washington, DC 20577
Telephone: (202) 623-1000 general
                (202) 623-6278 external relations

The bank holds free one-day briefings about four times a
year. For reservations, call (202) 623-1363. The contact for
the bank at the U.S. Department of Commerce may be
reached at (202) 482-1246.

African Development Bank

Headquarters:
01 BP 1387,
Abidjan 01
Cote d'Ivoire
Telephone: 011-225-20-44-44
Fax: 011-225-21-77-53

North American Office:
2001 Pennsylvania Avenue
Suite 350
Washington, DC 20000
Telephone: (202) 429-5160
Fax: (202) 659-4704

The U.S. Department of Commerce liaison contact for the bank may be reached at (202) 482-4333.

Asian Development Bank

P. O. Box 789
1099 Manila, Philippines

Street address:
6 ADB Avenue, Mandaluyong
Metro Manila, Philippines
Telephone: 011-63-2-711-3851
Fax: 011-63-2-741-7961

The Asian Development Bank does not have an office in the U.S. There is, however, a U.S. Department of Commerce liaison contact for the bank who can be reached at (202) 482-4333. The bank produces *ADB Business Opportunities,* a monthly publication to which you may subscribe at:

Subscriptions
Information Office
Asian Development Bank
P.O. Box 789
1099 Manila, Philippines

European Bank for Reconstruction and Development (EBRD)

One Exchange Square
London EC2A 2EH
Telephone: 011-44-71-338-6000
Fax: 011-44-71-338-6100

The EBRD does not have offices in the United States. There is, however, a U.S. Department of Commerce liaison contact who can be reached at 202-482-1246.

IV. INTERNATIONAL BUSINESS/ GOVERNMENT TRADE ORGANIZATIONS

These organizations are primarily concerned with promoting relations and commerce between their geographic regions and the United States, or among all member nations. Generally, the board of directors of such organizations consists of executives from the member companies in the United States. Some of these groups have similar organizations in foreign countries, and all are active in dealing with the relevant government officials and business leaders in the countries concerned.

These groups provide a ready and convenient channel to stay abreast of business issues in certain areas and to hear the concerns and interests of other business people involved in the regions. Because of the consolidated size and clout that a group represents, it also can have influence with the U.S. government or a foreign government in terms of advising on business/government issues of interest.

Council of the Americas

The area of focus is Latin America.

New York Office:
680 Park Avenue
New York, NY 10021
Telephone: (212) 628-3200
Fax: (212) 517-6247

Washington Office:
Suite 1200
1625 K Street NW
Washington, DC 20005
Telephone: (202) 659-1547

United States Council for International Business

1212 Avenue of the Americas
New York, NY 10036-1689
Telephone: (212) 354-4851

The Asia Society

Headquarters:
725 Park Avenue
New York, NY 10021
Telephone: (212) 288-6400

Washington office:
1785 Massachusetts Avenue NW
Washington, DC 20036
Telephone: (202) 387-6500

There are other offices in the U.S. The Asia Society seems
to work on all levels: cultural, political, and business.
It clearly seeks to promote understanding in all these
areas.

U.S.–ASEAN Council on Business and Technology

1400 L Street NW, Suite 650
Washington, DC 20005
Telephone: (202) 289-1911

The council focuses on the six members of ASEAN, Singapore, Malaysia, Indonesia, the Phillipines, Thailand, and Brunei.

World Economic Forum

53 chemin des Hauts-Crêts
CH-1223 Cologny, Geneva
Switzerland
Telephone: 011-41-22-736-0243
Fax: 011-41-22-786-2744

The forum promotes economic cooperation and worldwide prosperity by bringing together business, political, and academic leaders in confidential settings. It seems to be highly effective in its efforts and is a valuable resource for a quick personal introduction to the key players in the more difficult regions of the world.

Chambers of Commerce

The U.S. Chamber of Commerce in Washington can offer advice about contacts worldwide. There are of course offices of the U.S. chamber throughout the U.S. Abroad there are affiliated chambers known as American Chambers of Commerce. Further, there are in the U.S. several branches of foreign, non-U.S. chambers of commerce. There are books that list the various chambers and provide addresses and telephone numbers, described in the book section in this volume.

U.S. Chamber of Commerce
1615 H Street NW
Washington, DC 20062
Telephone: (202) 659-6000

Country-Specific Organizations

There are an enormous number of organizations specific to a particular country. Examples are the Venezuelan–American Association of the United States, Inc., or the U.S.–New Zealand Council. For your particular country of interest, you should ask the foreign embassy if there are such private business/government associations. The country desk offices at State and Commerce may also be able to lead you to them. Some are also listed in the books noted in the following section, especially the *International Business Practices* book.

V. READILY USABLE RESOURCE PUBLICATIONS

Below is a list of helpful books and other publications and their suppliers.

Government Printing Office (GPO)

The GPO is listed first as several of the publications recommended here may be obtained from its Washington office, or from its bookstores throughout the country. To order from the GPO, you should contact:

Superintendent of Documents
U.S. Government Printing Office
Washington, DC 20402
Telephone: (202) 783-3238

International Business Practices

Published by the Department of Commerce with the
assistance of Federal Express Corporation and Delphos
Corporation, this is a recent publication summarizing
valuable information on business practices, commercial
policies, exporting, foreign investment, taxation, and
more, for more than a hundred important countries. It
also lists beneficial contacts in the U.S. and foreign countries. The book can be obtained from the GPO.

Export Programs: A Business Directory of U.S. Government Resources

This is a highly valuable pamphlet for those interested in
exporting, and for anyone interested in the myriad areas
within the U.S. government that might be of help to a
business exporting to other countries. It was produced by
the Trade Promotion Coordinating Committee. The pamphlet lists all such organizations, provides a statement of
what each might do for a company, and provides telephone numbers for pursuing contacts. Even though the
focus is on exports, this pamphlet is definitely of value to
anyone involved in international business, is free, and can
be obtained from the Trade Information Center at (800)
872-8723.

A Basic Guide to Exporting

This book from the International Trade Administration in
the Department of Commerce provides data on aspects
of exporting for firms contemplating such steps. It is available from the GPO.

The Economist

Called a newspaper by some but a news magazine by others, this is to me the best publication covering the entire world on a weekly, up-to-date, and knowledgeable basis. If you subscribe to this short weekly publication and flip through it, you will soon know much about what is happening throughout the world in government and business. You will certainly become an expert among your peers. Subscriptions can be obtained by calling (800) 456-6086 in North America, excluding Colorado and Mexico; there you must call (303) 447-9330.

Almanacs and Travel Guides

If you go to a large bookstore and look in the travel or geographic sections, you will note a vast array of modern almanacs and guides dealing with various regions of the world. Several are published and updated frequently, and perusing one for countries of interest can give you a quick feel for them, and for problems that may be faced by citizens or foreigners who might wish to relocate there.

Chamber of Commerce Publications

The U.S. Chamber of Commerce International Division publishes several books useful to international business endeavors. Of particular note are the *Directory of American Chambers of Commerce Abroad* and the *Foreign Chambers of Commerce and Associations in the U.S.* These and others, many specific to a country or region, or to particular concerns, may be ordered from this address:

International Division/Publications
U.S. Chamber of Commerce
1615 H Street NW
Washington, DC 20062-2000
Telephone: (202) 263-5460

Also published annually by another source is the *World Chamber of Commerce Directory*, which lists offices of American Chambers of Commerce throughout the world, offices of foreign chambers of commerce in the U.S., and other valuable information such as U.S. embassies in foreign countries. The book can be purchased from:

World Chamber of Commerce Directory
P.O. Box 1029
Loveland, CO 80539
Telephone: (303) 663-3231
Fax: (303) 663-6181

International Monetary Fund (IMF) Publications

See the IMF in Appendix section III.

World Bank Publications

See the World Bank in Appendix section III

VI. OTHER RESOURCES

Universities

Nearby colleges and universities may have schools of business, international affairs, or something similar, in which there is a professor knowledgeable in your particular country of interest. The professor may actually be a citizen of that country and teach applicable courses. Such a contact can open a valuable door into the local community of people and information concerning the country.

Libraries

You or some member of your team should spend time in a modern library looking through recent articles written on your area of interest. With the aid of computerized periodical-search facilities, you can quickly scan publications of the past couple of years to see what is happening politically, what companies may be going into the country, what's been written on the economy, and more. Scan *The Economist, The Wall Street Journal, Fortune, Business Week, Forbes, The New York Times, The Financial Times,* and similar journals.

Employees of Your Own Company

If your company has more than a few employees, you may have on the payroll someone who is an immigrant from the country in which you are interested. This is highly likely for medium- to large-sized companies. Certainly, such a resource should not be overlooked. The person may not have the business skills to be part of the team evaluating entry possibilities but may have insight into

The World Is Your Market

the country and its culture and politics. As with the university connection, this employee may be a door for you into the local community of information and people regarding this country.

Executives in Other Companies

If you can determine another American (or Canadian or European) company that has an affiliate in the foreign land, you should seek to contact the relevant executive in the home office. (By relevant I mean the executive actually responsible for the operation.) If this company is not a competitor of yours, this executive will likely be forthcoming with advice and war stories, and you may receive early warning about issues that you might otherwise not have discovered until later in the game.

Relief Organizations

As noted, if a major relief organization is active in the nation you are considering, a conversation with an official familiar with the country may bring additional insights. Also, the potential of mutual help exists between the organization and your future business. If the country has soft currency and little hard currency available, at some point your business may find itself with abundant local funds that it cannot convert to hard currency and remit as dividends back to the home office. The relief organization, which will need local currency to pay its local workers, may be willing to give you hard currency offshore through an intermediary, in return for an attractive exchange rate for soft currency supplied in the country to the organization's operation there. This of course would have to be worked out in cooperation with the relevant banking authorities.

There are many such relief organizations; three are given here:

CARE
151 Ellis Street
Atlanta, GA 30303
Telephone: (404) 681-2552

Save the Children Federation, Inc.
54 Wilton Road
Westport, CT 06880
Telephone: (203) 221-4000

World Vision
919 West Huntington Drive
Monrovia, CA 91016
Telephone: (818) 357-7979

VII. RESOURCES IN THE FOREIGN COUNTRY

By this point, you know that my advice is to do homework before venturing off to the country itself. That research will produce contacts to be pursued in the country. Below are listed several contact points for when you or your company's team are on the scene. Most of this was covered in detail in Chapter 4 and elsewhere.

U.S. Embassy in the Foreign Country

Your discussions with the State Department can lead to your contact there arranging for you to meet with the appropriate persons in the U.S. embassy in the country. Certainly this meeting should take place, as the embassy personnel and officials can offer advice regarding people

you may meet. You may also want to consult embassy officials later in your visit to obtain their opinions regarding
meetings you have had.

Meetings with Officials of Foreign Governments

The embassy of the foreign government in the United
States may have advice for you about the agencies and
officials you should meet when in its country. They will
assist you in arranging such meetings before you depart.
Similarly, the U.S. embassy in the country should be consulted for advice and comments as to who should be consulted in the government.

Chamber of Commerce

As noted earlier, in many countries there is a local chapter
of the American Chamber of Commerce. You can determine that by calling the chamber in Washington or by
consulting one of the directories noted earlier. A meeting with the chamber in the country will give valuable
insights into the local business community and may also
provide promising leads.

Meeting with Top Managers of Local
Affiliates of Western Companies

During the visit, you should be certain to meet with a few
top managers of other local operations of American,
Canadian or European firms. If they are not your direct
competitors, they may provide valuable insights about
doing business in the country, and may offer suggestions
as to others with whom you should meet.

Local Counsel

Your legal advisors at home should be able to make recommendations about possible outside legal counsel in the country.

Banks

Similarly, major international banks should be able to offer suggestions about banking in the country; they may even have a branch there and can provide assistance to you through it. The major development banks may also have suggestions of persons with whom you should meet. If the IMF or the World Bank have staff in the country in question, you should seek to meet with them to discuss the situation there.

Accountants

Again, international accounting firms may be able to make recommendations about possible contacts or advisors for you in the country.

And So On!

The list of possibilities goes on and on. This really is the way things get done; all you have to do is to start.

VIII. FOR THE SMALLEST BUSINESS

The international world is open today to the smallest of businesses. If you are in a very small company with only a few employees, but believe you have a product that can be marketed successfully in the international arena, there is no reason not to try. All of this book is relevant to your interests and concerns, but if you are indeed small, your options for participating internationally are more limited than those available to larger concerns. You have the first two suggested alternatives for entering a country in Chapter 4: selling products made offshore to customers in the country, and (slightly more involved) selling into a country with the assistance of a local representative, or agent. Setting up a distributorship is probably outside the scope of your possibilities at this time, although if you are successful it could become a reality.

The following presents succinctly the steps you, the very small international marketer, should pursue to become involved in the international business world. There are references to items covered in this book, but this is a slimmed-down, quickly read recipe for getting involved. Before beginning, I would note that you always have one other option: You can simply have another firm handle your product internationally. In such a case, that company probably would be acting as an agent itself, although it might buy for resale. You may be able to locate such a firm by the same avenues listed here for your getting directly involved. Certainly, the trade association for your industry and the contacts noted in the U.S. Departments of Commerce and State are good resources. The Office of Export Trading Company Affairs in the International Trade Administration may be a source of information about such companies, as well.

Let's turn to the steps for the very small business, then. Telephone numbers for the contacts noted below, as well as additional descriptive information, are given in the other sections of the appendix.

DECIDING WHERE TO SELL

Perhaps you have an idea about what country might be a good market; say, one of your customers in the U.S. asks you to supply his overseas operation, and you wonder if you could not do much more from a base in that country. Or, perhaps you have no idea where you should attempt to sell your wares. Here is a way to proceed:

1. First, you need some quick, easy-to-obtain background information to assess your prospects. You should immediately call the Trade Information Center in the Department of Commerce and request the pamphlet *Export Programs: A Business Directory of U.S. Government Resources.* This is a good, convenient source of areas of possible help within the various agencies of the U.S. government. The center itself will provide information on the resources in the pamphlet. Second, you should call the Government Printing Office and order two books, *A Basic Guide To Exporting* and *International Business Practices.* Finally, you should subscribe to the *Economist.* With the above books and the weekly *Economist* to keep you posted on current events, you have a broad and quickly digested supply of material to get started.

2. The next step is to call the Department of Commerce trade specialists and ask for the one most nearly fitting your industry. This is a source of advice for contacts for exporting, and of suggestions about countries and markets to consider.

3. If you have specific countries in mind, call the Department of Commerce International Economic Policy country desk officers. They specialize in trade and economic aspects of particular areas.

4. A call to the Department of State to speak to the country desk officer is a good step at this point. Here you will get a briefing of the latest in the relations between the U.S. and the country and an indication of any possible problems. You may also receive other leads for information and suggested contacts.

5. You should certainly contact any trade associations that relate to your industry, to discuss possible markets. If a country you are considering has a branch of its own chamber of commerce in the U.S., this branch might be another good resource.

6. The Small Business Association (SBA) is another valuable contact to be made. The Office of International Trade is a contact point within the SBA; it has information on top-growing markets for certain products.

7. As described in Chapter 4, you should speak to any other businesspeople you know operating in the areas you are considering. Also, you should ask if your banker has any international contacts. Similarly, your outside counsel and accountant should be consulted. They may not be able to help, but ask.

8. Aside from all the help you receive from these contacts and publications, if you are not familiar with the basic financial instruments of international trade, you will need to obtain that expertise. If you have a treasurer or accountant, he might be the one to become familiar; nevertheless, this is going to be an essential element in your success interna-

tionally. Although you might buy the latest international financial textbook or attend a class at a nearby business school in international trade or finance, you most assuredly should also ask for help at a major bank having international operations. A banker will be able to explain to you basic instruments such as the letter of credit, which will become a valuable document to you. Seminars from the Export–Import Bank would also be of value.

SELLING IN THE COUNTRY

Although you may be led into the international market by a customer who goes overseas, if you are serious, you are going to need someone selling on the scene, all the time.

The easiest form of such representation is an agent—a representative who is not your employee but who represents your products in dealings with potential customers. The agent makes sales, but does not take a financial interest in the buying and selling. You pay this person a percentage commission on the sales, ideally only when sales are consummated. This agent probably is a knowledgeable, successful local businessperson who may also represent several other companies in their marketing efforts, especially if your business is very small.

Chapter 4 discusses how to find a partner, including an agent. Most of that applies here, except that because your business is very small, you may not have extensive time, staff, or funds to devote to finding the appropriate agent. The contacts in the Department of Commerce will be of help, as will contacts through the Chamber of Commerce. Also, the host country's embassy in the United

States may help you in this. After you have done all the research noted above, you should indeed consider contacting the embassy. There may be a consulate close to you, but it would be worthwhile for you to meet with people in the economics section of the country's embassy in order to ask your questions and get answers. These people really will help. Similarly, it would be good for you actually to meet with the contacts in Commerce, State, and the Chamber of Commerce.

Eventually, you will obtain leads. Then the question arises of whether you want to visit the country to meet the agent. I'd advise you to do so. If your business cannot afford this, perhaps you should wait a while before trying the international world. It may be that a potential agent is so prominent that he visits the U.S. for his own interests and can meet with you here. That is convenient, but you would nevertheless benefit from a firsthand appreciation of the market and environment into which you will be attempting to sell your products. Choosing a market and an agent is too important to let this all happen without your obtaining direct personal impressions.

If you decide to visit the country, to the extent possible you should follow the steps described in Chapter 4. The State and Commerce contacts can help you in arranging meetings in the country; so can your contacts in the country's embassy in Washington. Surely, you should visit the U.S. embassy in the country and talk long, seriously, and clearly with people in the commercial section about what you are trying to do and need to know. They will help; that is their job. Ask about the agent you are considering, and also ask for other suggestions. Be sure to see the local American Chamber of Commerce if there is one. You should also get your potential agent to show you around, give you his appraisal of the market, and perhaps even introduce you to a few potential customers. After all, you are trying to assess what he has to offer. As noted in Chapter 4, be wary of any political connections the agent may have.

There will eventually be the need for an agreement between your company and your agent. You should follow the caveats given in Chapter 4 for agreements with partners. Be sure to include an escape clause. All the concerns and advice in choosing the local partner cited there apply to you as well.

At some point you will finally have an agent and will get into business. I suggest you reread Chapter 5, focusing on the fact that in many lands, local currency cannot readily be converted into hard currency. Your control is through the financial devices under which you sell, and I recommend the irrevocable confirmed letter of credit, under which you do not ship until the letter is confirmed to you by a prime bank in the U.S. that works with the customer's bank in the country. Even if your market is a modern industrial country with attractive hard currency, you should consider using this letter until you are more knowledgeable in the credit reliability of your customers in the country. Another caution is that you should pay the commission to the agent; don't let this person collect and pay you.

There are programs of the Export–Import Bank of the U.S. that may aid you in your sales efforts. As described in Chapter 7 and elsewhere in the Appendix, the Eximbank provides financing to support foreign customers in their purchases of American goods. The bank gives short seminars about their activities, and you might consider attending. Also, the Overseas Private Investment Corporation (OPIC), described in the same chapter, will provide insurance against unusual political risks, which you might need depending on the country in which you are selling.

There are other groups as well that may be of benefit and are listed throughout the book, such as USAID, but these are the primary sources.

With all this information you are ready to get involved.
The best advice is to take it one step at a time. As you make
one international sale after another, your knowledge and
confidence will grow. Remember, each country is different. This is not a world consisting of two groups, the
United States and everybody else; it is a world of about two
hundred different countries.

IX. FOREIGN EMBASSIES AND BUSINESS DEVELOPMENT OFFICES IN THE U.S.

Foreign embassies are all located in Washington, D.C., although some of the larger ones also have consulates in
major U.S. cities. When making your initial investigatory
call, you should ask to speak to someone in the commercial or economics section. An embassy of a large country
will have an extensive staff, but many smaller-country
embassies have small staffs; from the outset you may be
talking with a senior diplomat. Do not be concerned
about this, as they are very interested in promoting their
home countries. You are why they are here.

In addition to these embassies and their consulates,
some countries also have trade-development offices in the
U.S. whose purpose is to promote and facilitate trade and
business between the U.S. and the country. Several of
these are given in the following embassy list.

Country	Embassy Telephone Number
Afghanistan	(202) 234-3770
Albania	(202) 223-4942
Algeria	(202) 265-2800
Argentina	(202) 939-6400
Australia	(202) 797-3000

Country	Embassy Telephone Number
Austria	(202) 895-6700
Austrian Trade Commission	(212) 421-5250
Bahamas	(202) 319-2660
Bahrain	(202) 342-0741
Bangladesh	(202) 342-8372
Barbados	(202) 939-9200
Belarus	(202) 986-1604
Belgium	(202) 333-6900
Belize	(202) 332-9636
Benin	(202) 342-0741
Bolivia	(202) 483-4410
Botswana	(202) 244-4990
Brazil	(202) 745-2700
Brunei-Darussulim	(202) 342-0159
Bulgaria	(202) 387-7969
Burkina Faso	(202) 332-5577
Burundi	(202) 342-2574
Cameroon	(202) 265-8790
Canada	(202) 682-1740
Cape Verde	(202) 965-6820
Central African Republic	(202) 483-7800
Chad	(202) 467-4009
Chile	(202) 785-1746
China	(202) 328-2500
Colombia	(202) 387-8338
Cote D'Ivoire (Ivory Coast)	(202) 483-2400
Costa Rica	(202) 234-2945
Cyprus	(202) 462-5772
Czech Republic	(202) 363-6315
Denmark	(202) 234-4300
Djibouti	(202) 331-0270
Dominican Republic	(202) 332-6280
Ecuador	(202) 234-7200
Egypt	(202) 232-5400
El Salvador	(202) 265-9671

Country	*Embassy Telephone Number*
Ethiopia	(202) 234-2281
European Community	(202) 862-9500
Fiji	(202) 337-8320
Finland	(202) 363-2430
France	(202) 944-6000
Invest in France Agency	(212) 757-9340
Gabon	(202) 797-1000
The Gambia	(202) 785-1399
Germany	(202) 298-4000
Ghana	(202) 686-4520
Great Britain	(202) 462-1340
British Trade and Investment	(212) 745-0495
Greece	(202) 667-3168
Grenada	(202) 265-2561
Guatemala	(202) 745-4952
Guinea	(202) 483-9420
Guinea-Bissau	(202) 872-4222
Guyana	(202) 265-6900
Haiti	(202) 332-4090
Honduras	(202) 966-7702
Hong Kong	(202) 331-8947
Trade Development Council	011-852-833-4333
	(in Hong Kong)
Hungary	(202) 362-6730
Iceland	(202) 265-6653
India	(202) 939-7000
Indonesia	(202) 775-5200
Ireland	(202) 462-3939
Industrial Development	
Authority	(212) 972-1100
Israel	(202) 364-5500
Italy	(202) 328-5500
Jamaica	(202) 452-0660
Japan	(202) 939-6700
Japan External Trade	
Organization	(212) 997-0400

Country	Embassy Telephone Number
Jordan	(202) 966-2664
Kenya	(202) 387-6101
Korea (South)	(202) 939-5600
Kuwait	(202) 966-0702
Laos	(202) 332-6416
Lebanon	(202) 939-6300
Lesotho	(202) 797-5533
Luxembourg	(202) 265-4171
Macau	
Office of the Governor, Directorate of Economic Services	011-853-562622 (in Macau)
Madagascar	(202) 265-5525
Malawi	(202) 797-1007
Malaysia	(202) 328-2700
Industrial Development Authority	(212) 687-2491
Mali	(202) 332-2249
Malta	(202) 462-3611
Marshall Islands	(202) 234-5414
Mauritius	(202) 244-1491
Mexico	(202) 728-1600
Micronesia	(202) 223-4383
Mongolia	(202) 333-7117
Morocco	(202) 462-7979
Mozambique	(202) 293-7146
Myanmar (Burma)	(202) 332-9044
Namibia	(202) 986-0540
Nepal	(202) 667-4550
Netherlands	(202) 244-5300
Netherlands Foreign Investment Agency	(212) 246-1434
New Zealand	(202) 328-4800
Nicaragua	(202) 939-6570
Niger	(202) 483-4224

Country	Embassy Telephone Number
Nigeria	(202) 822-1500
Norway	(202) 333-6000
Oman	(202) 387-1980
Pakistan	(202) 939-6200
Panama	(202) 483-1407
Papua New Guinea	(202) 745-3680
Paraguay	(202) 483-6960
Peru	(202) 833-9860
Philippines	(202) 483-1414
Poland	(202) 234-3800
Portugal	(202) 328-8610
Portuguese Trade Commission	(202) 331-8222
Qatar	(202) 338-0111
Romania	(202) 232-4747
Russia	(202) 628-7551
Rwanda	(202) 232-2882
St. Kitts and Nevis	(202) 833-3550
Saudi Arabia	(202) 342-3800
Senegal	(202) 234-0540
Sierra Leone	(202) 939-9261
Singapore	(202) 537-3100
Economic Development Board (EDB)	
New York	(212) 421-2200
Washington, DC	(202) 223-2571
Trade Development Board (TDB)	(212) 421-2207
Slovak Republic (Slovakia)	(202) 965-5160
Slovenia	(202) 828-1650
South Africa	(202) 232-4400
Spain	(202) 265-0190
Sri Lanka	(202) 483-4025
The Sudan	(202) 338-8565
Suriname	(202) 244-7488

Country	Embassy Telephone Number
Swaziland	(202) 362-6683
Sweden	(202) 944-5600
Switzerland	(202) 745-7900
Syria	(202) 232-6313
Taiwan (coordination council)	(202) 895-1800
China External Trade Development Council	(212) 730-4466
Tanzania	(202) 939-6125
Thailand	(202) 483-7200
Trinidad and Tabago	(202) 467-6490
Togo	(202) 234-4212
Tunisia	(202) 862-1850
Turkey	(202) 387-3200
Uganda	(202) 726-7100
Ukraine	(202) 296-6960
United Arab Emirates	(202) 338-6500
United Kingdom—See Great Britain	
Uruguay	(202) 331-1313
Venezuela	(202) 342-2214
Yemen	(202) 965-4760
Zaire	(202) 234-7690
Zambia	(202) 265-9717
Zimbabwe	(202) 332-7100

NOTES

INTRODUCTION:
THE NEW BUSINESS WORLD

1. For more information, see *The World Bank Atlas 25th Anniversary Edition* (Washington, DC: World Bank, 1992), 23.

CHAPTER 1: LOTS OF CHOICES:
RANKING THE COUNTRIES
IN ATTRACTIVENESS

1. The annual real economic growth percentages are gross domestic product percentages based on

information from: *International Financial Statistics Yearbook* (Washington, DC: International Monetary Fund, 1992), 149–51; *The World Bank Atlas 25thAnniversary Edition* (Washington, DC: World Bank, 1992), 18–19; *Handbook of International Statistics, 1992* (Washington, DC: Central Intelligence Agency, 1992), 16–26; *Inter-American Development Bank 1992 Annual Report* (Washington, DC: Inter-American Development Bank, 1993), 2; and conversations with country embassies in Washington, DC., and the U.S. Department of Commerce.

2. For more information, see *Growth and Ethnic Inequality, Malaysia's New Economic Policy* (New York: St. Martin's, 1990).

3. "Provisions of 1990 Immigration Act," *Congressional Quarterly Almanac, 101st Congress* (Washington, DC: Congressional Quarterly, Inc., 1991), 482.

4. See this chapter, note 1. "Germany" refers to the former West Germany in this table.

5. Ibid.

6. See "How Motorola Took Asia by the Tail," *Business Week*, no. 3239 (November 11, 1991), 68.

7. See this chapter, note 1.

8. "Hungary to Learn," *The Economist*, 326, no. 7804 (March 27, 1993), 72.

CHAPTER 2: JUST HOW DIFFERENT?

1. *World Bank Atlas*, 8–9.
2. Ibid.

CHAPTER 3: HOW MUCH ALIKE?

1. *World Bank Atlas,* 18–19.

CHAPTER 7: HOW TO FINANCE

1. See *The World Bank Annual Report, 1992* (Washington, DC: *World Bank,* 1993), 4–5 and throughout for further description of the World Bank's role and activities. Also see *World Bank Atlas,* 36.

2. See *1992 International Monetary Fund Annual Report,* (Washington, DC: International Monetary Fund, 1992), 53–54 and throughout for further description of the IMF's role and activities.

3. See *Inter-American Development Bank 1992 Annual Report,* page opposite title page and throughout for more description of the bank's role and activities.

4. See any of several bank publications, such as *How to Work with the European Bank for Reconstruction and Development* (London: European Bank for Reconstruction and Development, 1991). Also see Ibrahim F. I. Shihata, *The European Bank for Reconstruction and Development: A Comparative Analysis of the Constituent Agreement* (Boston: M. Nijhoff, 1990), 41, 60–61.

5. See *African Development Bank Group in Brief* (Abidjan, Cote d'Ivoire: African Development Bank Group, 1993) for a fuller discussion of the objectives and functions of the bank group.

6. See any of numerous background publications by the bank, such as *Basic Information* (Manila, Asian Development Bank, 1993), and *Questions and Answers,* (Manila, Asian Development Bank, 1990).

7. See *Export–Import Bank of the United States Annual Report 1992* (Washington, DC: Export–Import Bank of the United States, 1993), page 1 and throughout for a discussion of the Bank's role and activities. Also, see short releases from the Bank's office of public affairs: "Export–Import Bank Fact Sheet," April, 1993, 2 pages; and "Eximbank Services for Small Business," March, 1993, 4 pages.

Chapter 8: Who Are You Competing With?

1. "East Europe for Sale," *The Economist,* 315, no. 7650 (April 14, 1990), 15–16.

Chapter 9: Unique Opportunities

1. See Phyllis Berman, "Contrarian Investing 101," *Forbes,* 151,1 (January 4, 1993), 68–69 for a fuller discussion.

2. "A Latin Big Bang," *The Economist,* 326, no. 7798 (February 13, 1993), pages S16–S17.

3. "Argentina's Oil Company Going Public," *New York Times,* 28 June 1993, pages D1 and D8.

4. "Going Private," *The Economist,* 328, no. 7821 (July 24, 1993), 5.

CHAPTER 11: THE ROLE OF GOVERNMENT

1. See Carla Rapoport, "Why Japan Keeps on Winning," *Fortune*, 124, no. 2 (July 15, 1991), 76–85, for a discussion on *keiretsus*. For more on *keiretsus*, see Marie Anchordoguy, "A Brief History of Japan's Keiretsu," *Harvard Business Review*, 68, no. 4 (July–August, 1990), 58–59.

2. See "Chapter Four: Foreign Corrupt Practices Act" in *International Business Practices* (Washington, DC: U.S. Department of Commerce, January 1993), 17–18. Also, *Congressional Quarterly Almanac, 95th Congress* (Washington, DC: Congressional Quarterly, Inc., 1977), 414.

CHAPTER 13: SECURITY: THE BUSINESS, THE EMPLOYEES, AND YOU

1. See Berman, "Contrarian Investing 101."

CHAPTER 14: ENVIRONMENTAL ISSUES WILL FOLLOW YOU ANYWHERE

1. For more background, see "The Question Rio Forgets," *The Economist*, 323, no. 7761 (May 30, 1992), 11–12. Also, see "The Green Legacy," *The Economist*, 323, no. 7763 (June 13, 1992), 39–40.

Index